Essential Bulgaria

by
DAVID ASH

David Ash has toured Bulgaria extensively on visits since 1962, when he was one of the first western travel writers to cover the country's emergent tourism.

Following 13 years as travel editor of the *Daily Express*, he has written freelance for a variety of national publications, including *Country Life* and the *Daily Telegraph*.

AA

Produced by AA Publishing

Written by David Ash
Peace and Quiet section
by Paul Sterry

Edited, designed and produced by
AA Publishing. Maps © The
Automobile Association 1994

Distributed in the United Kindom by
AA Publishing, Fanum House,
Basingstoke, Hampshire,
RG21 2EA.

The contents of this publication are
believed correct at the time of
printing. Nevertheless, the
publishers cannot be held
responsible for any errors or for
changes in details given in this
guide or for the consequences of
any reliance on the information
provided by the same.
Assessments of attractions, hotels,
restaurants and so forth are based
upon the author's own experience
and, therefore, descriptions given in
this guide necessarily contain an
element of subjective opinion which
may not reflect the publisher's
opinion or dictate a reader's own
experience on another occasion.
We have tried to ensure accuracy
in this guide, but things do change
and we would be grateful if
readers would advise us of any
inaccuracies they may encounter.

First published 1990
Revised Second Edition © The
Automobile Association 1994.

A CIP catalogue record for this book
is available from the British Library

ISBN 0 07495 0833 7

Published by AA Publishing, which
is a trading name of Automobile
Association Developments Limited,
whose registered office is Fanum
House, Basingstoke, Hampshire,
RG21 2EA.
Registered number 1878835.

Colour separation: LC Repro,
Aldermaston

Printed by: Printers Trento, S.R.L.,
Italy

Cover picture: *Shipka Memorial*
Church

Country Distinguishing Signs

On the maps, international distinguishing signs indicate the location of countries around Bulgaria:

ⒼⓇ = Greece
ⓇⓄ = Romania
ⓉⓇ = Turkey
ⓎⓊ = former Yugoslavia

This book employs a simple rating system to help choose which places to visit:

✓ 'top ten'

◆◆◆ do not miss
◆◆ see if you can
◆ worth seeing if you have time

INTRODUCTION

*Near Cape
Kaliakra, on the
Black Sea coast*

INTRODUCTION

Bulgaria is still largely one of Europe's best-kept tourist secrets despite its claim to be its oldest nation state. Just north of Greece and Turkey, east of the former Yugoslavia and south of Romania, it contains a great variety of attractions in addition to the sunny Black Sea beaches and the ski resorts best known to holiday-makers.

About four-fifths the size of England but with a population of only nine millions, scenically it boasts several mountain ranges for winter sports and summer recreation, fertile plains, the Valley of Roses, the Danube and lesser rivers, ancient cities and hill villages, monasteries and churches with painted icons, mosques, Roman and Thracian antiquities, modern and long-established health spa resorts, the parks and metropolitan features of Sofia, and much more.

These have virtually all been open to foreign visitors for years. But since 1989 and the change from Communism to democracy, the country more actively encourages a greater diversity and ease of travel arrangements.

Since 1957, Bulgaria has planned mass tourism amenities more whole-heartedly – more professionally, some might say – than have many other Eastern European countries.

Achievements

Being the satellite which traditionally had the closest links with the Russians (through language and culture, and the Russians' liberation of Bulgaria from 500 years of Ottoman domination), it is thought to have had a freer hand to 'do its own thing' in tourism – and with remarkable achievements for a nation whose troubled history had reduced it to little more than a backward peasant economy not many years ago.

For inclusive tours or individually arranged holidays, the Black Sea's large or small resorts – with reliable sun from April through October,

clean golden-sand beaches and safe bathing – variously cater for families with children, the youth market, the over-55s, those seeking extra comforts or reasonable luxury in hotels, self-catering villa clients, guests in village rooms, or 'basic' campers.

Holiday atmosphere is lively, especially in ski resorts where, incidentally, instructors speak *and* understand English well after intensive courses in the language. There is plenty of varied nightlife including discos and folk-style restaurants, but not the 'wild' scene of some Mediterranean areas. The Bulgarian coast is 235 miles (378km) long, with vast sandy beaches, large bays and rocky shores. The sea is clean, without tides, predatory fish or dangerous animals. The sand bottom slopes gently, making it suitable for small children. Together with the requirements of many tour operators, Bulgaria's economic costings have perhaps led to a superficial and unfair view of Bulgaria as just another cheap-and-cheerful sun/sand/sea destination for the packaged masses (though not, so far, drunken and rowdy elements). But there is much more to this 'unexplored' country than at first appears.

Culture and Heritage

Culturally, Bulgaria has an importance disproportionate to its size, and especially in music and ballet. Where else can a *world-class* opera performance be attended at rock bottom prices? Its choirs are among the very best anywhere, and Sofia's May/June Music Weeks attract the cream of international orchestras and soloists.

Musicality has been strong from earliest times. The southern Rhodope mountains gave rise to the legends of Orpheus, his lyre and his poems. And today a haunting song from that region (see Shiroka Luka, pages 63-64) is travelling beyond our planet aboard *Voyager*. 'Peasant' traditions, are very much alive and kicking in regional varieties and give package tourists folklore performances that can be more vividly authentic than commercially contrived efforts elsewhere. There are also unique displays by troupes of fire-walkers. It may surprise some to learn how much

Bulgaria's turbulent history is frequently commemorated by monuments. Above, near Aitos

Bulgarians venerate their monasteries – there are at least 120 – and churches. Whether or not they are believers, they acknowledge the role of the Christian religion in the early founding of their State and its culture, and its often active support in campaigns against oppression by (for instance) Ottoman occupiers. Many religious buildings, their art treasures and devotional symbols, are carefully preserved.

Wining and Dining

Bulgaria's fresh salads and fruits are memorable, as are the stews with multiple vegetables and herbs, slowly casseroled in earthenware dishes. Its name is virtually synonymous with ewesmilk yoghurt that is the best in the world. Its wines now enjoy an international reputation for quality and value. Anyone who has regarded them as outlandish novelties did not know, presumably, that the Thracians were enjoying local wine hereabouts 2,400 years ago and more – as evidenced in the amazingly preserved murals of a tomb near Kazanluk.

People and Politics

Socially, most Bulgarians have a friendly disposition – it seems even jollier and more ebullient as one travels southwards – and they are now, post-Communism, even less likely to be inhibited about talking to foreign visitors. The police are helpful, as far as language permits. Certain laws, which may affect the tourist, are, however, strictly enforced. 'Wild camping', on unscheduled sites, is not allowed, and it is illegal to drive with any alcohol in the blood, or without your driving licence. Cars at border points may be searched; Bulgaria is on the east-west drug traffic route, and customs officials have to be diligent. Photographing military installations is not permitted, nor is unofficial money-changing – always use banks or exchange bureaux.

Balkantourist guides are usually efficient, helpful and knowledgeable. They do *not* drone on about record productivity in tractor plants and collective farms. Just a little extra patience, and a sense of respect, may be needed by a tourist who is unused to visiting countries outside the usual EC range of holiday destinations.

There will be a great variety of other attractions and diversions – sometimes in places which seem unpromising at first sight.

Archaeology

The Thracians, the Hellenes, the Romans and the Byzantines contributed to Bulgaria's archaeological monuments. There are many remnants of monumental buildings, public baths, tombstones, sculptures, fortification walls and coins.

Among the masterpieces of ancient art in the country are the murals of the Thracian Tomb at Kazanluk (4th century BC), the Gold Treasure of Panagyurishte, the Gold Treasure of Vulchitrun, and the Silver Treasure of Lukovit. Bulgaria also has numerous monuments from the period of the Bulgarian Khans and kings.

Architecture

There are interesting ruins at the former capitals of Pliska and Preslav, and the beautiful National Revival buildings at Rila, Bachkovo and Troyan monasteries, and in the towns of Koprivshtitsa, Kotel and Zheravna. Plovdiv and Veliko Turnovo have both important archaeological remains and fascinating old quarters.

More recent architecture can be seen in the buildings of the National Assembly, Ivan Vasov National Theatre, the mineral baths building, market hall and the National Museum in Sofia, theatres in Ruse and Varna, and others throughout Bulgaria.

Organised Holidays

For those who prefer an organised holiday with a theme, various companies (see the **Directory**) offer special interest holidays, from agricultural or architectural tours to wild fruit gathering or ornithology.

For the active tourist there are walking holidays, high mountain tours, donkey trekking, hunting, fishing, horse riding, sports camps, tennis courses and folk dancing.

For the artistic there are courses in handicrafts, pottery, sculpture, woodcarving, poker-work,

Veliko Turnovo, a picturesque town in a picturesque setting, has carefully preserved its older buildings

Bulgarian rug making, painting, drawing, icon painting and photography.

For the gourmet there is herb gathering, mushroom picking, wild fruit gathering, cookery courses, canning of fruit, wine making and tastings.

There are trips by narrow gauge railway, and by cart along the mountain roads. Festivals include the June Rose Festival in Kazanluk and Karlovo, the Trifon Zarezan Vine Growers Festival in February, the March Music Days in Ruse, the Sofia Music Weeks in May and June, Lilac Music Celebrations in Lovech, the Festival of Humour and Satire in Gabrovo, folklore festivals in Burgas and Rozhen, the 'Pirin Sings' folklore festival, and many other varied and interesting events throughout the country.

HISTORICAL BACKGROUND

The first people that the historian can name as living in the lands that became Bulgaria were the Thracians, who, with their highly developed culture, founded colonies on the Black Sea coast. The Thracians were fine horsemen and these, and other animals, are depicted on the magnificent tomb finds made in Bulgaria. Eventually the Romans stretched their yoke as far as the Black Sea by subduing the Thracian tribes. Christianity first arrived when the Roman Emperor Constantine made it the official cult of his realms. Even when the northern barbarians finally demolished the remnants of administration flowing from Rome at the beginning of the 5th century AD, the land remained part of the Greek-speaking Roman world under emperors ruling from Constantinople.

But waves upon waves of heathen tribes were pouring down from the north and east: Avars, Slavs – and the Bulgars, who were to give the land the name it still bears.

The Bulgars crossed the Danube towards the end of the 7th century AD and in 681 Khan Asparoukh founded the first Bulgarian State, with a blending of Slavs. Early in the 8th century this was independent of the Byzantines and controlled the land between the Balkan Range and the Carpathian Mountains.

Relics from the ancient civilisations of the area may be seen in Sofia's Archaeology Museum

Violent Acts

It was at its most powerful at the beginning of the 9th century when a Bulgarian Tsar captured a Byzantine Emperor, had his head chopped off and ordered a drinking cup to be made from the skull.

The Bulgars and Slavs became Christian later in the century when their prince, Boris I, was converted by the brothers Cyril and Methodius – also renowned for devising the Cyrillic alphabet still used in Slav languages.

The Bulgars' power was destroyed in a battle in 1014 which culminated in more outrageous violence. The Byzantine victor Basil II took more than 15,000 prisoners, blinding all but 150 whom he left with one eye each, to guide the defeated blind army back to the Bulgarian Tsar. The point was taken, and Bulgaria became a province of the Byzantine Empire shortly afterwards. But the Byzantine Empire had its problems – attacks not only from the former barbarians from the north but from the ever-present Arabs.

So the Bulgarians, after a series of unsuccessful

Turbulence and conflict: the war between the Serbians and the Bulgarians, 1885

uprisings, were able to break away again in 1187. This Second Bulgarian Empire was to last for more than 200 years and become the strongest state in southeast Europe; stretching from the Black Sea to the Mediterranean and taking in modern-day Hungary and the former Yugoslavia.

The Tatars plundered from the north and the Arabs pressed from the south, but it was internal strife that divided this Empire into three separate kingdoms which finally fell, one by one, to the Ottoman Turks. Muslim domination was to last for five centuries, yet the individual culture, customs and religion of the Bulgarians survived.

The Eastern Question

It was this strong cultural identity that sustained the Bulgarians through the long, slow decline of the Ottoman Empire from the end of the 17th century. The Great Powers bolstered up the Sultans for their various reasons – Britain because her diplomats were obsessed with protecting her trade routes to India. All were suspicious of Russia, the rising star of the Slav nations, who might take the spoils of rotting Turkish rule.

Slav nationalism., inspired by the publication in 1762 of Father Paissi's Slav-Bulgarian History, grew – but only slowly among the illiterate peasants of Bulgaria.

Many Russians supported Pan-Slavism – and the idea that it was natural for the oppressed Slav peoples to come under the protection of Russia. Bulgarian volunteers fought for Russia in several successful wars against the Turks. But when the Turks refused the Russian demand to protect Christians within the Turkish Empire, the 'Eastern Question' sparked off the Crimean War, with Britain, France and Austria coming to the aid of Turkey, the 'Sick Man of Europe'.

Russian Action

After Russia's retreat, the Bulgarian national liberation movement grew. In April of 1876 they rose against their oppressors. This uprising was suppressed with such ferocity that the whole of Europe was shocked. The Turks armed irregular Muslim troops who fought for loot and slashed their way through 60 villages killing everyone in sight.

In Britain, Gladstone spoke in Parliament of the Bulgarian horrors and the public began to wonder just why its government supported a nation capable of the massacre of 30,000 men, women and children.

A conference was called in Constantinople but nothing was decided. The Turks refused to accept reforms.

So Tsar Alexander II of Russia declared war on Turkey in April 1877 'to preserve the dignity and honour of Europe'. Eventually, helped by Bulgarian volunteers and other oppressed Slavs, the Turks were defeated.

The San Stefano Peace Treaty, signed on 3 March 1878, set up (among other things) a Bulgarian independent state. But the Great Powers had plans to divide the Turkish Balkans more to their advantage.

A new peace conference was called resulting in the Treaty of Berlin. This divided Bulgaria into three, restoring the southern part to

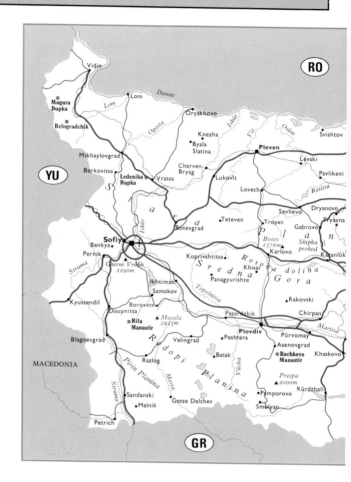

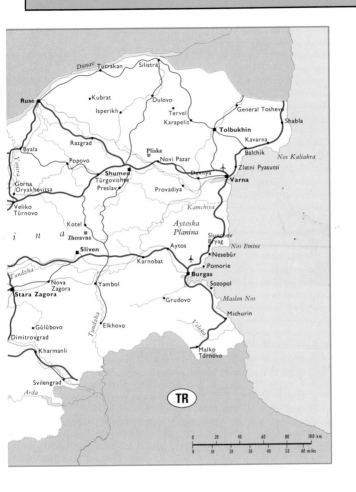

Turkish rule. The Bulgarians were angry but set about looking for a constitutional ruler and imported a German prince, Alexander of Battenburg.

The Smouldering Balkan Fuse

Western diplomats knew that the unsettled state of the Balkans was an issue that threatened the delicate balance of power in Europe. Bulgarians, unhappy with the Berlin treaty, realised that friendly big brother Russia did not favour her eventual union with Roumelia, the former Ottoman possession which had incorporated Thrace together with Macedonia and Albania. Moreover, their new prince was forced to accept Russian generals as ministers. In the south the Roumelians revolted in September 1885, and in spite of Turkish protests even Britain would soon recognise the new union. Bulgaria appeared to have reached a precarious independence.

Then the Serbs declared war on Bulgaria in November, were defeated smartly, but were rescued when the Austrians threatened to intervene. The Russians added to the heated situation by supporting an army kidnap of Prince Alexander, forcing him to abdicate. He came back, but the Tsar refused to accept him and the Bulgarians had to look for another prince. They found Prince Ferdinand of Coburg and in the teeth of opposition from the Russians voted him in in 1887.

Relations with Russia only became amiable again after the death of Alexander III. When the baby heir of Ferdinand was baptised into the Orthodox Church in 1896 Tsar Nicholas II stood as godfather. In 1897 both the neighbouring big powers, Austria-Hungary and Russia, had accepted the status quo.

Rise of Socialism

Bulgaria was to remain a monarchy until the end of World War II, but the economic developments that came with independence brought industrialisation and the foundation of a politically active proletariat.

In 1891 the Bulgarian Social Democratic Party, which later became the Communist Party, appeared, and the Bulgarian Agrarian Union was set up in 1899.

An independent Bulgaria was able to make its own alliances and in 1912 agreed with Serbia that Macedonia should become Bulgarian. Later in the year it was also allied with Greece and Montenegro in fighting the Turks in the first Balkan War.

In the second Balkan War she fought both Serbia and Greece, was attacked by Romania and lost most of what she had gained.

Sporadic violence marked the early years of Bulgarian independence – here the attempted assasination of Prime Minister Stromboli

Le Petit Journal

TOUS LES VENDREDIS
Le Supplément illustré
5 Centimes

SUPPLÉMENT ILLUSTRÉ
Huit pages : CINQ centimes

TOUS LES JOURS
Le Petit Journal
5 Centimes

Deuxième Année   SAMEDI 18 AVRIL 1891   Numéro 21

LES ÉVÉNEMENTS DE BULGARIE
(Assassinat de M. Beltchef en présence de M. Stambouloff)

World Wars Role

Bulgaria declared itself neutral when World War I broke out. Britain offered her Macedonian territory to join the Allied side but in 1915 she allied herself with Germany and attacked Serbia. In the fighting that followed Bulgaria defeated a British and French army who were then bottled up in Salonica. Greece declared war on Bulgaria.

When the Allies' offensive began in Macedonia the Bulgarians were themselves defeated. In the peace of Neuilly they lost valuable territory and had to pay heavy indemnities.

A Peoples' Republic

After a period of Agrarian government, a right-wing *coup d'état* in May 1923 brought a Fascist dictatorship which retained a king to keep the peasants happy.

In September of 1923 the first Communist rising, led by Georgi Dimitrov and Vassil Kolarov, was brutally suppressed. Between the wars Bulgaria suffered severely from economic depression and support for the Communists gradually increased.

When World War II started Bulgaria again declared neutrality but in 1940, with German help, regained some land it had lost to Romania during the Balkan Wars. In March 1941 it associated itself with the Axis, and in a few days was occupied by German troops. Bulgaria declared war on Britain and the US in December of the same year.

In 1942 Dimitrov, the Communist leader, set up the Fatherland Front, an organisation of progressive and democratic forces against Fascism. A mass anti-Fascist uprising started, that ended in the overthrow of the monarcho-fascist government on 9 September 1944. The government of the Fatherland Front was formed. In 1946 Bulgaria became a People's Republic.

Under the leadership of Todor Zhivkov, who came to power in the mid-50s, Bulgaria eagerly toed the Soviet party line. Then, in the late 80s, Communism crumbled throughout the whole of Europe, including Bulgaria, and Zhivkov was ousted. Elections in 1991 gave victory to the UDF (democrats).

SOFIA (SOFIYA)

Sofia today would surprise anyone who may still vaguely visualise Bulgaria as an insular peasant state. Its population was only 20,000 in 1878, the year before it was declared capital of the country newly liberated from the Turks. Now the population has increased 60-fold to1.2 million, it has hosted sessions of UNESCO and the World Tourism Organisation in its vast Palace of Culture, and is starting to be recognised for the fascinating city that it is.

Thus it can claim to have stuck to its motto: 'To grow but not to age'.

Its outer suburbs extend to the foothills of Mount Vitosha (Cherni Vrukh), whose peaks rise to a maximum 7,500 feet (2,290m). It builds and refurbishes hotels in partnership with western and Japanese corporations. But it carefully preserves its native trees, its antiquities, and musical traditions – ranging from folkloric to operatic and symphonic in the annual International Sofia Music Weeks held during May and June. Culture comes with a formal capital C in at least 20 museums and galleries, 14 dramatic and opera stages, eight concert halls, five permanent exhibitions, 57 cinemas, and scores of historical, architectural and commemorative monuments. There is no notional equivalent in the city of London's Soho,

The Ivan Vasov National Theatre in Sofia, a city whose cultural life is held in high regard

SOFIA

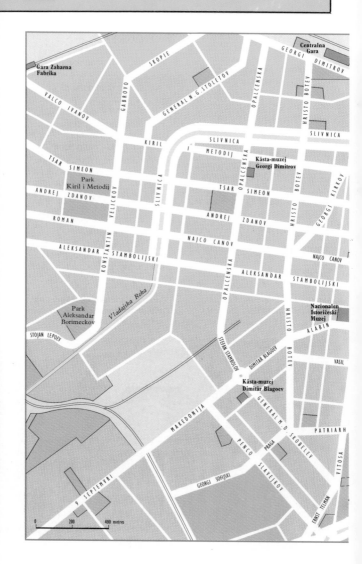

Centralna Gara

Gara Zaharna Fabrika

GEORGI DIMITROV

SKOPIE

VALCO IVANOV

GABROVO

GENERAL N G STOLETOV

OPALCENSKA

HRISTO BOTEV

KIRIL

SLIVNICA

I METODIJ

SLIVNICA

TSAR SIMEON

Park Kiril i Metodij

SLIVNICA

VELICKOV

OPALCENSKA

Kåsta-muzej Georgi Dimitrov

TSAR SIMEON

BOTEV

GEORGI KIRKOV

ANDREJ ZDANOV

HRISTO

ANDREJ ZDANOV

ROMAN

KONSTANTIN

NAJCO CANOV

NAJCO CANOV

ALEKSANDAR STAMBOLIJSKI

ALEKSANDAR STAMBOLIJSKI

OPALCENSKA

Park Aleksandar Borimeckov

Vladajska Reka

Nacionalen Istoriceski Muzej

HRISTO

ALABIN

STOJAN LEPOEV

STEFAN STAMBOLON

DIMITÅR BLAGOEV

BOTEV

VASIL

Kåsta-muzej Dimitår Blagoev

GENERAL M D SKOBELEV

PATRIARH

MAKEDONIJA

PENCO

PRAGA

SLAVEJKOV

VITOSA

GEORGI SOFIJSKI

9 SEPTEMVRI

ERNST TELMAN

0   200   400 metres

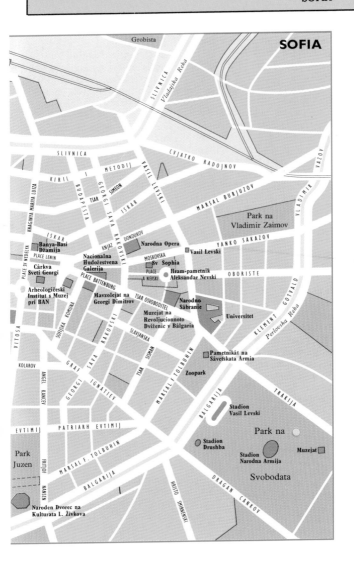

SOFIA

Grobista

SLIVNICA
Vladajska Reka

CVJATKO RADOJNOV

SLIVNICA

KIRIL I METODI

KNIAGINYA MARIJA LUIZA

BUDAPESTA

GEORGI SAVA RAKOVSKI

TSAR SIMEON

ISKAR

VASIL LEVSKI

MARSAL BURJUZOV

Park na
Vladimir Zaimov

VLADIMIR

JAZOV

ISKAR

**Banja-Basi
Džamija**
PLACE LENIN

**Cǎrkva
Sveti Georgi**

**Arheologičeski
Institut s Muzej
pri BAN**

PLACE SV NEDELJA

**Nacionalna
Hudožestvena
Galerija**
PLACE BATTENBERG

KNIAZ DONDUKOV

Narodna Opera

MOSKOVSKA

Sv Sophia
PLACE
A NEVSKI

**Mavzolejat na
Georgi Dimitrov**

TSAR OSVOBODITEL

YANKO SAKAZOV

Vasil Levski

**Hram-pametnik
Aleksandar Nevski**

OBORISTE

**Narodno
Sǎbranie**

**Muzejat na
Revoljucionnoto
Dviženic v Bǎlgaria**

Universitet

KLEMENT GOTTWALD

Pernovska Reka

VITOSA

SOFIJSKA KOMUNA

SLAVJANSKA

GRAF SAVA

RAKOVSKI

TSAR

SIOMAN

MARSAL TOLBUHIN

**Pametnikǎt na
Sǎvetskata Armia**

KOLAROV

ANGEL KANCEV

GEORGI IGNATIEV

Zoopark

TRAKIJA

BALGARIJA

**Stadion
Vasil Levski**

EVTIMIJ

PATRIARH EVTIMIJ

FATJOV

NANSEN

**Park
Juzen**

MARSAL F. TOLBUHIN

BALGARIJA

**Stadion
Drushba**

Park na

**Stadion
Narodna Armija**

Muzejat

Svobodata

DRAGAN CANKOV

HASTO SMIRNENSKI

**Naroden Dvorec na
Kulturata L. Živkova**

New York's Greenwich Village, the Paris Left Bank, or the Croisette in Cannes (with which Sofia shares roughly the same southerly latitude). Discos offer fairly standard western/international rock/pop. Après-ski in the Vitosha resorts, however, is likely to be as lively as in almost any winter sports area. And there is quite an animated atmosphere at numerous bars and restaurants – some national and folkloric, some with overseas cuisines – in Sofia and in the summer resorts on the Black Sea coast.

History

From ancient times the Sofia plain was a crossroads for east-west and north-south migrations, as indicated by its early name: Sredets (centre). Archaeological excavations locally have yielded traces of civilisation from 7,000 years ago. In the 8th century BC the Thracian tribe of Serdi settled here, giving way to the Romans and their town Serdica. After standard demolition work by Attila the Hun's hordes, this was rebuilt in the 6th century by the Byzantine Emperor Justinian. In 811 it was conquered by the incoming Bulgarian Khan Krum (whose name now graces labels on bottles of sensationally good. cheap Bulgarian Chardonnay) and incorporated into the First Bulgarian State. Following re-occupation by the Byzantines, as Triaditsa, it was annexed into the Second Bulgarian Kingdom by Tsar Ivan Shishman in a 14th-century deed which had the first known reference to the name Sofia.

The Ottomans captured it in 1382 after a long siege, and did not finally leave hold until the Russian General Gurko entered Sofia with his troops in January 1878.

Heavily bombarded in 1944, it was a centre of Communist resistance to the Fascist regime, which ultimately capitulated on the Ninth of September.

WHAT TO SEE IN SOFIA

ROMAN FORTRESS WALLS

These walls have been found by archaeologists and are now on view in a city-centre pedestrian underpass at the lower ground floor of the Sofia department store, and at Exarch Yossif Street.

The **Western Gate of Ancient Serdica** is to be found on Sveta Nedelya Square, and the **Northern Gate** is under the Central Supermarket on the Largo.

ROTUNDA OF ST GEORGE

Aleksandar Stambolijski Boulevard

In a courtyard behind the Sheraton Hotel Balkan, finely preserved, 4th-century. There are also remains of a 2nd-century street and other antiquities.

ST SOPHIA CHURCH

Parizh Street

The 4th to 6th-century church has survived intact, down to 1,600-year-old mosaic details of trees, flowers and birds.

◆◆◆
ALEXANDER NEVSKY
MEMORIAL CHURCH ✓

The Alexander Nevsky Memorial Church, as resplendent inside as out

Alexander Nevsky Square
Between Moskovska Street and the handsome Tsar Osvoboditel Boulevard that is lined with several rows of horse chestnut trees. Completed in 1912 as a tribute to the Russians who died in the 1877–78 Russo-Turkish war, liberating the country from Ottoman rule. This massive golden-domed chuch is the most splendid of many notable buildings from around the turn of the century. Craftsmen and artists from six countries worked for 30 years on the five-aisle church, which can accommodate 5,000. The glow from huge chandeliers and candelabra illuminates 82 icons, 273 mural paintings, and the finishes of marble, onyx, alabaster, gold, copper and bronze.

Downstairs in the crypt of the church is a notable collection of icons and religious artifacts dating back hundreds of years. Services, especially at Eastertide, offer a magnificence of singing and spectacle.

◆◆◆
THE NATIONAL
HISTORY MUSEUM ✓

2 Vitosa Boulevard
The world's oldest known gold
artefacts were found in
Bulgaria, as were the Thracian
gold treasures of Vulchitrun

*A display of souvenirs of Sofia
which reflects the country's
traditional crafts*

and Panagyurishte. Items of
these can be seen in this
important museum, sometimes
in reproduction if the originals
are 'on tour' for exhibition
elsewhere. Its ground floor
houses a wealth of rare objects
ranging from the Palaeolithic
Age to the 14th century AD,
which may account for an hour
before the visitor contemplates
the next floor and its detailed
illustration of the centuries of

the Turkish Yoke and the National Liberation Movement.
Open: Tuesday to Thursday, Saturday and Sunday 10.30 to 18.30
Closed: Monday and Friday morning

◆
THE NATIONAL ARCHAEOLOGICAL MUSEUM
2 Aleksandar Stambolijski Boulevard
In the former Buyuk Mosque, the National Archaeological Museum has exhibits of the tribes and peoples of Bulgaria from antiquity to the 19th century.
Open: 10.00 to 12.00; 14.00 to 18.00
Closed: Monday

◆◆
THE NATIONAL ART GALLERY
Battenburg Square
Housed in the former royal palace, the gallery features a collection of Bulgarian pictures from the 19th and 20th centuries. The Ethnographic Museum is in the same premises, but this may be closed for renovation.
Open: 10.00 to 18.00
Closed: Monday

◆
FORMER MAUSOLEUM OF GEORGI DIMITROV
Battenburg Square
This used to be guarded by sentries in old-style dress uniform, roughly the symbolic equivalent of Lenin's Tomb in Moscow's Red Square. Dimitrov's body was removed in 1990; the site is now closed, awaiting a new role.

Entertainment
An important place for entertainment in Sofia is the **National Palace of Culture**, at the south end of Vitosa Boulevard. Built to mark the 13th centenary of the creation of the Bulgarian State, this modern complex is an ambitious building. It is an established congress centre. Set in new public gardens with fountained ornamental ponds, it is claimed it can accommodate 16,844 people participating simultaneously in some kind of activity. Its central hall has several thousand seats, and there are a dozen other halls attached, with hi-tech facilities and infrastructure, 160,000 square feet (15,000 sq m) exhibition space, restaurants, café, and shops.
It can rise quite efficiently to the big occasion. But massive congresses of world bodies like UNESCO do not happen every week, and it might seem that there is scope here for western incentive-conference organisers to negotiate extra-competitive rates.
At theatres, performances are naturally most likely to be in Bulgarian. There may occasionally be Shakespeare in the vernacular.

Shopping
Shopping Centres: TSUM (the Central Department Store), the Largo, stocks western imports (credit cards accepted). **Halite** (the Markets), Khyaginya Mariya Luiza Boulevard.
Zornitsa, Vitosa Boulevard.
Valentina, in the triangle between Graf Ignatiev, Sofiiska Kamouna and Alabin Streets,

and on Vitosa Boulevard. **Denitsa**, in the underpass of the Central Railway Station.

Speciality Stores: Bulgarski Houdozhnik (applied art works), 6 Tsar Osvoboditel Boulevard (credit cards accepted). **Bulgartabac**, 2 Tsar Osvoboditel Boulevard. **Vitex** (fabrics), 29 F Nansen Boulevard; 28 Tolbukhin Boulevard. Quartz (crystal, glass and china ware), 35 F Nansen Boulevard; 8 Vitosa Boulevard (credit cards accepted). **Mineralsouvenir** (articles and gifts made of marble and semi-precious stones, jewellery), 10 Tsar Osvoboditel Boulevard.

Mladost (sports articles), 1 Positano Street and 18 Ivan Assen II Street. **Pamoukotex** (cotton fabrics and ready-to-wear), 33 F Nansen Boulevard. **Peroun** (fashions), 42 Dondukov Boulevard. **Pirin** (footwear and leather wear), 4 Slavyanska Street; 19 Vitosa Boulevard; 86 Vitosa Boulevard; Stambolijski Boulevard. **Rila** (ready-wear), 63 Vitosa Boulevard; 35 Vitosa Boulevard and 52 Vitosa Boulevard. **Rouen** (knitwear), 50 Alabin Street; 34 Tolbukhin Boulevard (credit cards accepted).

Typical cuisine – simple, natural and healthy

Corecom shops, usually in hotels, used to sell cigarettes, spirits, watches, perfumes, etc, at prices below those of duty-free shops at west European points of departure. Once strictly for hard currency, leva are now accepted at the few remaining shops.

Eating Out
When callng from outside Sofia, preceed telephone numbers with the code 02.

Bulgarian Folk-style Restaurants
Goroublyansko Hanche, Goroublyane suburb; *Mehani* (taverns) in the larger city

The Viennese café, one of the restaurants in the 1930s-style Sheraton Hotel Balkan, Sofia

hotels; **Koprivshtitsa**, in the Trade Centre on Vitosa Boulevard; **Zheravna**, 26 Tolbulkin Boulevard; **Rozhen**, 74 Vitosa Boulevard, serves specialities from the southern, Rhodope region, eg: *cheverme* (tender spit-roasted lamb), *drob-sarma* (rice with mutton, liver, spices and egg), large white Smolyan beans (can produce a 'Blazing Saddles' wind effect), *Katchamak* (fried maize-flour cakes served with cheese). At **Bulgarska Gozba**, 34 Vitosa Boulevard, (tel: 879162) there is a fair variety of Bulgarian dishes on offer. As the restaurant is situated on a very busy thoroughfare, it gets crowded quickly, so booking is always advisable. You can sit

outdoors or inside – the ambience is relaxed and informal. The **Garden Club** in Positano Street has very stylish decor, and a good standard of Bulgarian food with excellent service.

Other National Cuisines: At **Krim**, 2 Dobroudja Street (tel: 870131), you can eat outdoors in the summer, the menu is Russian, the prices high for Sofia, and the tone very refined. You could also try **Havana** (Cuban), 27 Vitosa Boulevard; **Budapest** (Hungarian), 145 Rakovski Street; **Berlin** (German), Yanko Sakazov Boulevard; **Warszawa** (Polish), Yanko Sakazov Boulevard, **Vietnam** (Vietnamese), 1 Georgi Kirkov Boulevard; **Forum** (French), 64 Vitosa Boulevard; **Pyeong Jang** (Korean), 24 A Zlatarov Street.

Restaurant Complexes: Rubin, Sveta Nedelya Square; **Kristal**, 10 Aksakov Street; **Coop**, Vitosa Boulevard; **Forum**, 64 Vitosa Boulevard; **Havana**, 27 Vitosha Boulevard, and at the National Palace of Culture.
Cafés: Prolet, 21 Tsar Osvoboditel Boulevard; **Kristal**, 10 Aksakov Street; **Magoura**, 80 Vitosa Boulevard; **Sportna Sreshta**, 17 Tolbukhin Boulevard.

Accommodation
Sheraton Sofia Hotel Balkan, 5-star, Sveta Nedelya Square (tel: 876541). A characterful thirties-style establishment carefully refurbished to Sheraton standards; chandeliered conference rooms, restaurants, tavern, coffee lounge, nightclub,

fitness centre.
Vitosha New Otani, 5-star, Anton Ivanov Boulevard (tel: 62451). Spacious, high-rise, hilltop, calmly modern international-style luxury with plenty of daylight; Sakura Japanese restaurant, Lozenets Bulgarian restaurant, day and night bars, variety bar and casino, fitness centre, indoor swimming pool and sauna, bowling, tennis court, shops.
Rodina, 4-star, 8 Tsar Borisov III Boulevard (tel: 51631). High-rise, with deluxe features but possibly depressing taste in dark-brown modern ceilings. Good restaurants and banquet halls, bars, shops, bowling, swimming pool, sauna.
Novotel Europe, 4-star, 131 Knyaginya Mariya Luiza Boulevard (tel: 31261). High-rise, modern/functional style; restaurants, lounge bars, night clubs, conference halls, shops.
Grand Hotel Sofia, 3-star, 3 National Assembly Square (tel: 878821). Opposite the Parliament and other august buildings, giving a feeling of where it's all at, modern and not highly stylised; lofty, airy main restaurant, night club with floor show, tavern, coffee lounge, bars, Triaditsa hall for business meetings.
Park Hotel Moskva, 3-star, 25 Nezabravka Street (tel: 71261). Restaurants and banquet halls. Panorama restaurant, snack bar, night club, coffee lounge, day bars, Russian restaurant with floor show, conference halls, shops.
Bulgaria, 3-star, 4 Tsar Osvoboditel Boulevard (tel: 871977).

Hotel Shtastlivetsa in Cherni Vrukh, Bulgaria's highest ski resort, just half an hour from Sofia

Hemus, 3-star, 31 Georgi Traikov Boulevard (tel: 661415).
Slavia, 2-star, 2 Sofiiski Geroi Street (tel: 525551).
Slavyanska Besseda, 2-star, 127 Rakovski Street (tel 883691)
Serdika, 2-star, 2 General Zaimov Boulevard (tel: 443411).
Pliska, 2-star, 87 Trakiya Boulevard (tel: 71281)
Convenient for airport passengers; restaurant diners serenaded by music.

Tourist Offices
See page 119.
Street plans of Sofia are available at tourist offices, major hotels, car rental offices, etc.

EXCURSIONS FROM SOFIA

◆
ISKUR GORGE
Northwards from Sofia, the road from Novi Iskur to Lyutibrod follows the winding Iskur Gorge, carved out by the fast-flowing River Iskur.
The walls of the gorge are spectacular rock formations, sometimes so steep and close that – from the passenger seat of a car or train (on the Sofia–Mezdra line) you have to look up vertically at their summits, looming up to 800 feet (250m). Eroded by weather and water, some resemble canyons in the North American Rockies. Others, with symmetrical terracing and cloud-piercing pinnacles, would make a theatrical backdrop for some

Wagnerian epic.

Partially grey limestone, the strata are seamed at intervals with 'stripes' of other rock – a diagonal band of yellowish colour, then a parallel one above it of dusky pink hue. About halfway between Novi Iskur and Svoge (a town with coal mining and other industry) a right turn leads off 2.5 miles (4km) to the village of Batuliya, whose railway halt is named **Tompsan**. This commemorates Major William Frank Thompson, member of a British mission aiding Bulgarian partisans who died in a 1944 battle with the gendarmerie.

Beyond Lakatnik, where the canyon rocks are particularly impressive and popular with climbers, is the village of Cherepish, near whose railway halt is the **Cherepish Monastery**. This is a 14th-century foundation restored in the 16th century and again in the 19th, after being ravaged several times during the Ottoman occupation.

RITLITE ROCKS

Just west of the small town of Lyutibrod. Three parallel walls of outcrop rock ranging down over hill contours into the valley. Though known locally as 'Cart Rails', from a distance they also look strikingly like man-made fortified ramparts whose watchtowers and turrets have been knocked about a bit.

CHERNI VRUKH, DRAGALEVTSI, BOYANA

The number 66 bus from the Hladilnika tram stop on Sofia's Vitosa Boulevard, bound for the Shtastlivetsa Hotel in Cherni Vrukh, reaches **Dragalevtsi**, in the wooded foothills, within 15 minutes.

At lunchtime, alight at the Vodenicharski Mehani – preferably on a weekday, when there is not such heavy booking at this folk-style restaurant, converted from three 200-year-old water mills. Specialities here include *katchamak* (fried maize dough) with meat, and a *shish-kehab*, skewered meat and onion grilled and flamed with vodka. There is often folk music.

DRAGALEVTSI MONASTERY

Frescoes here date back to the 14th century when it was founded by King Ivan Alexander. About 2 miles (3km) further near a number 66 bus stop.

Boyana and its celebrated church, nestling at the foot of Mount Cherni Vrukh, can be reached by bus from Sofia. The Balkantourist office, 1 Vitosa Boulevard will give details.

◆◆
BOYANA CHURCH

Begun in the 11th century, it contains frescoes from 1259 which are claimed to be among the best-preserved and most interesting examples of Eastern European medieval art.

Some of the 90 scenes are painted from life rather than stylised. The picture of the Last Supper contains typical early Bulgarian detail, including the people's everyday fare of garlic, radishes and bread and traditional clothes worn by the locals of the time.

At a stop 20 minutes' drive further the **Zlatni Mostove** area (3,900 feet/1,200m) is reached. Surrounded by forests, it has a restaurant quite near the curious 'stone river' of boulders strewn by early flood torrents of extinct glaciers.

ALEKO VITOSHA

The highest of Bulgaria's ski resorts, Aleko on Mount Cherni Vrukh lies at 6,129 feet (1,868m) with skiing up to 7,415 feet (2,260 m), so the season lasts reliably from early December until late spring. The mountain forms a backdrop to Sofia, just half an hour's bus ride from the

The exquisite Turkish drinking fountain in Samokov, dating from the 17th century

slopes. Cherni Vrukh's lifts rise high above the treeline and the slopes are long and steep enough for most skiers. The slopes are mainly north-facing and can be windy (except where they descend into the protecting treeline) but they are never icy. Cherni Vrukh at the highest point gives wonderful views over the whole region. Vitoshko Lale, the run down from Cherni Vrukh, is the blackest and most difficult in Bulgaria. There is also a steep wall, Stenata, which is particularly challenging, and the whole area is good for training. A four-person chairlift, a triple, a double and several draglifts give a total uplift of 7,000 skiers an hour.

EXCURSIONS FROM SOFIA

This means that queues, even when a proportion of the million inhabitants of Sofia decide to ski, are kept to a minimum. Classes are grouped according to language, for Cherni Vrukh is very international. Skiers come from Germany (German and Russian are commonly spoken in Bulgaria); and from other European countries as far apart geographically as Greece and the Netherlands.

The village of Aleko is small and purpose-built. You can ski from the door of the Hotel Shtastlivetsa and back again to it at the end of the day. It has a big sun terrace, from which to watch skiers returning after the challenge of the day. The Prostor hotel is more luxurious, with its own small swimming pool, nightclub, sauna and solarium. It is often used by holiday companies for package ski trips.

Prices are reasonable in all the Bulgarian resorts and Cherni Vrukh has a special flavour for those who have only skied in western resorts. The proximity of Sofia offers sightseeing and shopping possibilities and the ski area will keep all the enthusiasts in the party happy. It is possible to stay in Sofia and travel out to the slopes daily.

The sheer Ritlite rocks in the Iskur Gorge, a winding canyon sculpted by the River Iskur

THE NORTHWEST

VRATSA and LEDENIKA DUPKA

Vratsa stands near the foot of Kamarata mountain, where Hristo Botev, Bulgarian guerrilla leader, hero and poet, was killed by Turkish troops after a hard battle in the early uprisings of 1876. It has a theatre, history museum and art gallery.

From April to October the Balkantourist office at 21 Georgi Dimitrov Street can direct sightseers to The Lift (so called locally) – a funicular whose chairs will carry them above wooded hillsides to the 2,700 feet (830m) high pastures in which is the entrance to the Ledenika (Icicle) Cave. This is a 20-minute, 1.5 mile (2.5 km) ride; low-season alternative is a 10-mile (16km) taxi or car ride up a southwesterly road signposted to Ledenika.

◆
LEDENIKA DUPKA

Limestone complex formed 2.5 million years ago by water action. Its floodlit caverns include the 'Concert Hall', 197 feet (60m) by 148 feet (45m) and 75 feet (23m) high, whose excellent acoustics encourage the Vratsa Philharmonic Orchestra and/or famous choirs to perform programmes in it on special occasions. Normally, the only sounds in the caverns are the echoes of visitors' voices, the slow drips of stalagmite-forming water and the occasional hissing of (harmless) bats hanging from the cave roof.

Electric lighting shows up stalagmite formations perceived fancifully as giants, Jack Frost, the Madonna, Santa Claus, elephant, octopus, and the hut of the Slav witch Baba Yaga. Cave temperatures drop from a summer 40°F (4°C) to something well below freezing in winter, when water penetrating the roof causes opaque ice formations which brilliantly reflect the spotlighting. In pre-refrigeration days, silkworms were stored in an upper, moderately cold cavern. Warm clothing is an obvious necessity, as are non-slip shoes for the damp walkways. There is a basic café near the entrance.

Open: Virtually year round, 08.30 to 16.00; 45-minute tour.

Eating Out/Accommodation

Hotel Hemus, 2-star (tel: 092 23581), with restaurant, pastry-shop, bar and 'beer-pub'.
Hotel Balkan, 1-star (tel: 092 24469), with restaurant.
Hotel Hashore, 2-star (tel: 092 27570), with restaurant. Accommodation at the **Hotel Tourist** is intended mainly for members of the Bulgarian Hikers' Union (BTC) but its restaurant is apparently open to all. Comfortably furnished, it offers good value for money.

BERKOVITSA

Berkovitsa is an old-established town producing wines from locally grown strawberries, raspberries and blackcurrants. It has a warren of narrow streets and several museums. On the northern slopes of the

Balkan range, 12 miles (20km)
west of the spa resort of
Vurshets (or Varsec) and 15
miles (24km) southwest of
industrial Mikhaylovgrad,
Berkovitsa boasts a mild climate
and is being developed as a
mountain resort.

Among local sights are **The
Clock Tower** of 1762, the
**Virgin Mary (Sveta
Bogoroditsa) Church** and its
artistic contents, the **Kaleto hill
fortress** and early Christian
basilica remains, and the
Gramada, 2 miles (3km) out by
the road to Mikhaylovgrad – a
pile of stones which grew over
many years as a symbol of anti-
Turkish sentiment; each one
thrown with a hearty curse.

HOUSE OF IVAN VAZOV
This is the home of the revered
writer of *Under the Yoke* and
other chronicles of struggles
against the occupying Turks.

Eating Out/Accommodation
Hotel Mramor, 2-star with
restaurant.

Balkantourist Office, 1
Berkovska Komuna Square.

BELOGRADCHIK ROCKS
Some of the strangest natural
sights in Europe are the rocks
and gorges in an 18 mile
(30km) by 2 mile (3km) area
around Belogradchik, a small
town a short distance along a
left turn off the E79 road
northwest from Mikhaylovgrad.
Often more massive than the
most grandiose of Bulgaria's
man-made monuments, they
are sometimes over 500 feet
(150m) high and have

reminded travellers of solitary
obelisks, many-towered castles,
giant representations of
historical figures, or mythical
beasts sculpted by nature.
Set amongst winding gullies or
leafy wilderness, they led a
19th-century traveller to
enthuse: 'The famous Oliul
gorges in Provence, the

The Belogradchik fortress, built into a fairy-tale world of rock formations resembling animals, people and castles

Pancorbo defile in Spain, the Pyrenees, the Alps... all these are incomparable with what I saw near Belogradchik in Bulgaria!'

An asphalt road now enables motorists to drive up to a fortress, built high in the rocks, with various accretions from the 1st century to the 19th century.

Accommodation
Hotel Belogradchik Rocks, 2-star.
Madonna campsite with bungalows.

◆
MAGURA (MAGOURA) CAVE
Magura Cave, (near Rabisha, west off the E79 road at Dimovo), is one of the most interesting of Bulgaria's many natural caverns because of its evidence of prehistoric human habitation and its mysterious rock 'paintings'. These are daubings with bat guano, a dark brown substance so durable that it has preserved the area of rock covered by the 'paintings' – which thus stand out in relief.
Some archaeologists have dated them back merely to the beginning of the Bronze Age (2,700BC). But another school of thought suggests they are as much as 17,000 years old – which may be nearer the mark if the animal pictures were anything like authentic reproductions. They seem to include creatures somewhat like giraffes, ostriches and even kangaroos, which might only have existed in this region at an early time when its climate was much hotter.
Human figures include hunters with bow and arrow, dancing women (in grass skirts?) and men.
One of the 'halls' nearer the cave entrance contains remains

of a fireplace, clay pots, and other items from almost 3,000BC, while another cavern has been variously used by Bulgarian freedom fighters since the 19th century.
The most massive of the stalagmite formations may be nearly 3 million years old. As in other caves, they are taken to resemble buildings, trees, and human or animal figures when floodlit. Live resident bats still drop guano. The cave is very extensive, and a tour can take an hour and a half. A short walk down the hillside from its entrance, which gives views over the large Rabisha Lake, is a simply furnished *mehana* (tavern). This serves excellent minced meat balls (*kyufte*) plus inexpensive house wines or the pink Magura champanska which is fermented by *methode champenoise* in a bottle and stored in the cave. The town base for visiting Magura, and Belogradchik Rocks, might well be Vidin.

VIDIN

Vidin is a major port on the Danube, at the northernmost point of the E79 highway. Linked by ferries to the factory town of Calafat on the Romanian bank, and to a wooded river island, it appears from southern approaches to be more mundanely industrial than touristic until you reach the area around the medieval Baba Vida fortress, built on riverside foundations of a Roman fort from the 3rd to 4th century BC. However, there are aspirations to make Vidin a duty free area – presumably with some

upgrading of its amenities, though its hotels currently meet demand as unpretentious bases for local sightseeing and jaunts out to Magura Cave and Belogradchik Rocks.
A new theatre under construction in Vidin is intended to be 'the most modern in Bulgaria'. And a Vidin district

Vidin, a major centre

product which can hardly be bettered anywhere for zestful value is the famous red Gamza wine of Novo Selo, a village in its northwest corner between the borders of Romania and the former Yugoslavia.

◆◆
THE BABA VIDA FORTRESS
Impressively preserved towers, ramparts and (since the occupying Turks sometimes met a lot of resistance here) former prisons, death cells and a scaffold stand in park-like surroundings. Some of its vintage cannons were made in England. It contains a museum, and in summer provides an outdoor theatre for its 'Shakespeariad' (though its historical plays are not always Shakespeare's). Periodically it

is used as a film set, and it often attracts archaeologists.

◆
THE DISTRICT HISTORY MUSEUM

A short walk away from the Baba Vida Fortress, in the 18th-century Krustata (cross-shaped) Barracks, the museum features items from the agricultural past to the acrylic-fibre and water-pump producing present. It is currently being given a face-lift.

◆
KONAK

Displays earlier arts and crafts in its archaeological museum. Most items on display are artefacts from the Roman era.
Open: 09.00 to 12.00 and 14.00 to 18.00

Closed: Monday

Accommodation
The **Hotel Rovno**, 2-star (tel: 94 24402), in the town centre, has a reasonable restaurant, a bar with music, and a friendly enough welcome.
The Bononia, 2-star, 4 Bdin Street (tel: 94 23031), has restaurant, bar, and snack-bar.
The **Nora Pizanti Campsite**, 1-star, run by the Union of Bulgarian Motorists, is out on the road south to Sofia.

Balkantourist Office,
Dondukov Street (tel: 94 24976).

Rila Monastery's wealth of frescoes make it the country's most important monument from the National Revival period

THE SOUTHWEST

◆◆◆
RILA MONASTERY

Rila Monastery (Rila Manastir) is
the most famous of Bulgaria's
seven major monasteries (there
are quite a number more), and
a prime example of work from
the National Revival Period,
with 1,200 beautifully
preserved wall paintings.
The stern stone building is
3,500 feet (1,100m) up in a leafy
valley of the Rila Mountains, 74
miles (119km) from Sofia on an
east turn off the E79 from
Kocherinovo. Its central fortified
Tower of Hrelyo (1335) is the
only surviving medieval
portion. The monastic
community was founded in the
10th century, and continues its
devotions today. A full-bearded
priest glides around its
colonnaded courtyard,
hammering out summonses to
prayer on a wooden sounding-
board. Visitors light prayer
candles in its Holy Virgin
Church, which glows with
murals by Zahari Zograph and
other National Revival artists.
The museum has a vast
collection of ancient documents,
painted icons, fabrics,
jewellery, carvings, carpets and
metalwork from all over the
country, a cross sculpted by the
monk Raphael with a needle
contains 140 biblical scenes,
with 1,500 tiny human figures,
which he completed in 1802,
after 12 years – at the cost of his
eyesight. The library contains
20,000 old books.
One of the nine Bulgarian
landmarks on UNESCO's
protection list, Rila Monastery
was awarded the International
Federation of Travel Journalists
Golden Apple Prize in 1980.

Accommodation
The **Hotel Rilets**, 3-star, just
west of the monastery, has 14
single rooms, 64 doubles and
five suites.

◆◆
BANSKO
Bansko is a museum town with
period houses, native place of
several famous Bulgarians, and
year-round mountain resort in
the 87-peak Pirin range with
lakes in the vicinity. It is 25
miles (40km) east of Simitli on
E79.
In spring and early summer its
slopes can be iridescent with
wild flowers such as tiger lilies,
globe flowers, alpine poppies
and (high up towards the 9,560
foot, 2,914m, Vihren peak) Pirin
edelweiss.
Now being developed for
winter sports, it has good snow
from early December until
March, and there has even
been talk of local skiing in
August. There is a 5,000-foot
(1,500m) long ski run, with two
1,100-foot (330m) beginners'
courses, ski drags and a semi-
stationary electric drag.
Sons of Bansko include Paissi of
Hilendar, the 18th-century
monk whose important
Bulgarian History helped to
buoy up nationalist spirits, and
Nikola Vaptsarov, the anti-
Fascist poet who was executed
in 1942 and whose house is
now a museum. In cobbled
streets are National Revival
houses with fascinating façades,
windows and eaves.

Eating Out/Accommodation

The **Pirin Hotel** (tel: 7443 2295 or 2536) has a restaurant, plus a tavern serving national dishes, bar, discothèque, and tourist office. There are restaurants and other facilities on the main Georgi Dimitrov Boulevard.

◆◆◆

MELNIK

The smallest town in Bulgaria, but rich in interest, Melnik is scattered along a gorge flanked by tall and very neatly eroded canyon rocks, in pale gold sandstone.

Apart from its unique topography, it is famous for its dark red wine of dense gravity (it was reputedly once so thick that 'you could take it away in a cloth').

Melnik is best visited from Sandanski, along an east

Melnik's houses nestle in a deep valley against a backdrop of sandstone pyramids

turning 5 miles (8km) south down the E79. Founded by the Thracians and Slavs, in ancient times it was a crossroads for travellers between the eastern Mediterranean and lands to the east and north. The Romans and Byzantines left their marks. Around the turn of the 12th century, Melnik was the capital of the despot Alexii Slav, who ruled much of the Rhodopes and Struma region. In the 17th and 18th centuries Melnik flourished and grew with its wine and tobacco trade, eventually to a population of 14,000 with 74 churches. It declined in the late 19th century, and much of it was destroyed in the later Balkan war. But it retains the shell of its 10th to 11th-century '**Boyar's House**' and numerous well preserved houses of the National Revival Period, their jettied upper storeys supported by fine beams.

Especially notable is the 1754 **Kordopulov House**, atop a steep cobbled path towards the village's inner-gorge extremity. It is now a museum, with intriguing furnishings and extensive wine cellars tunnelled into bedrock.

In the street below, opposite an ancient bath house, are impressive houses including one whose owner may invite you in to his cellar, where his own red wine is an alternative to that sold at the cosy bar by the huge plane trees in what is roughly the town centre.

Eating Out

The **Chinarite Mehana**, just opposite, serves good chicken soup, meatballs and salad, with Melnik red wine.

Accommodation

On the same side of the gorge, built almost against a cliff, is the **Melnik Hotel,** 2-star (tel: 272), newish but in architecture meant to be sympathetic, for visitors who would savour local atmosphere longer – and perhaps before the regular coach parties arrive.

◆
SANDANSKI SPA

Sandanski is a leading health centre, with a mild Mediterranean-type micro-climate, mean annual temperature of 58°F (14°C) and the purest of air, claimed to be

---

Son of Sandanski

Spartacus was said to have come from what is now Sandanski, and he was a healthy enough Thracian to have overpowered a gladiator or two while leading the slaves' revolt against the Romans in the 1st century BC. Whether or not he looked like Kirk Douglas in the Hollywood epic you can check at his statue by the entrance to the town, 104 miles (166km) south of Sofia on E79.

---

the best in Europe for bronchial and respiratory problems (a counter-blast, perhaps, to the effects of tobacco, of which Bulgaria is a major and high-quality producer).

Its slightly mineralised hot springs, ranging from 100° to 160°F (37° to 72°C) at source, are used in the hydro of the ultra-modern 4-star Sandanski Hotel for treatment of kidney conditions, gastritis, colitis, and inflammations of the skin – as well as in the hotel's pools. Also dealing with arthritic, muscular, gynaecological and nervous complaints, the hydro additionally offers electric treatment, paraffin wraps, electric ionotherapy, acupuncture, light treatment, inhalations, herbal medicine, massages, and remedial exercises in gymnasia.

Thus it attracts quite a clientele of west Europeans who find the treatments and holiday cost of living much less expensive than in their own countries.

However, even travellers with less receptive national attitudes to hydrotherapy could find Sandanski, with its walks through wooded parkland, a pleasant base for excursions into the scenic Pirin mountains and to such fascinating villages as Melnik (see pages 40–1) and Rozhen (see below).

Accommodation
There are two hotels here to choose between: the luxurious **Hotel Sandanski** (tel: 0746 2106), whose versatile band can cater for the music/dance tastes of numerous nationalities over dinner. But those wanting another brandy after 22.00 when the main bar may close, should either stay in the restaurant or join the scrum waiting to be let in to the downstairs disco. (300 rooms) The **Spartak Hotel**, 2-star (tel: 0746 2045), has 27 single and 50 double rooms, seven suites, restaurant, bar, night club and coffee shop.

Balkantourist Office 28 Georgi Dimitrov Street (tel: 0746 2098).

ROZHEN
Cockerel crow and donkey bray greet the visitor to Rozhen. It is a village more truly rural and less self-consciously touristic than is Melnik (see page 40), though it is in a similar sandstone gorge just to the north.

Its houses have a sometimes rickety charm. Their wooden balconies are festooned with red peppers, gourds, pumpkins, and geraniums, their unruly kitchen gardens shaded by vines and murmuring with the lazy drawl of hens. Rozhen

village may not be a prime cultural monument of the National Revival Period, with UNESCO recognition. But it has memorable atmosphere.

Eating Out
The **Rozhen Mehana** does inexpensive meat balls (there is a choice: with or without onion) and local wine in an earthenware jug and mugs. Lively southern badinage may compete with the outlandish pop music on the bar's video television.

ROZHEN MONASTERY
Just beyond Rozhen church, Rozhen Monastery (Rozhen Manastir) is about a mile (1.5km) up and along a track which gives views of the gorge. Built in the 12 and 13th centuries, it is noted for its carved altar and lecterns, for paintings of monks and hermits apparently unknown anywhere else, and for its very early calligraphy school. Externally, it looks rather like an outsize version of a Rozhen farmhouse. A shopping bag, hung in a tree just outside its walls, may contain a large earthenware pot full of lunch for the monks.

SAMOKOV
Southwest of Sofia, Samokov may look prosaic now, but it fostered famous 19th-century schools of master craftsmen and artists – and it has a singular mosque and a decorated 17th-century Turkish drinking fountain, both just opposite the bus station. It lies 6 miles (10km) north of Borovets winter resort, it is

roughly halfway along the road linking Doupnitsa on E79 and Ihtiman on E80. It can be reached in a 38-mile (62km) drive south from Sofia along the road via Pancharevo which follows the Iskur valley through wooded mountain-and-lake country – particularly colourful in autumn.

The **museum** in the main square traces histories of iron founding, printing, etc. The **Belyova Church** contains many murals by painters from Samokov, whose sons included leading icon painters like Zahari Zograph.

◆
BAIRAKLI MOSQUE
Designed and internally decorated by Bulgarian artists who presumably also painted house and monastery interiors, and who here managed to reach a friendly compromise with Muslim worshippers about the use of various motifs which did not strictly accord with Koranic tradition that favours abstract designs.

The old part of this town, which had the first workers' commune in the Balkans, features the church of St Nicholas, with weathercocks on its roof.

BOROVETS
Borovets is set in the Rila Mountains about an hour and a half's drive from Sofia. The old kings of Bulgaria – deposed

Walking in the scenic Rila mountains, a popular area for hikers as well as skiers

after the last world war – had a hunting lodge here. Several mansions, built by the aristocracy, still lie back from the village road, now turned to hotels and hostels. As a ski resort it provides a fair challenge to intermediate skiers and opportunities for slalom training on the steep slopes. The village is attractive and facilities for families with young children are good.

The pine trees grow tall and broad (*Bor* is Bulgarian for pine) in these southern climes, and those slopes which are south-facing can get a bit patchy late in the skiing season, but the snow is usually reliable between December and the end of March because the lifts rise so high. The Musala range of the Rila Mountains has hosted many world cup ski races . The ski-school offers four hours' instruction a day, six days a week and caters especially for beginners but also up to advanced and race-training standard. Classes are videoed and once a week there is a video evening. There is a long green nursery slopes 'road' which any beginner can tackle successfully, a sheltered bowl under Mount Musala and the longest run in Bulgaria. The recent addition of a four-man chairlift to the existing 3-mile (5km) gondola, chairlift and many draglifts, gives plenty of uplift between 4,340 feet (1,323m) and 8,399 feet (2,560m) and opens up three separate small areas. Evening entertainment includes wine-tasting evenings, and folklore with traditional music and

dancing. The **Rila Monastery** is a fascinating relic of the past and well worth a day's visit (see page 39).

Eating Out/Accommodation

A few years ago experts from the French resort of Les Arcs were called in to design a new hotel called the **Rila**. This provides all the comfort and convenience usually only found in more western resorts. There are three restaurants, including a taverna for traditional Bulgarian food and a two-storey, fast-food café. The nursery for children up to four years of age operates 24 hours a day. From the age of three, children can join the kindergarten and learn to ski. The Rila has two- and three-bedded rooms, each with private bathroom. There is a gym, a sauna and an electronic games room.

There are, of course, other hotels, including the **Club Hotel Breza** reserved for Balkan Holiday clients; the Hotel Samokov, the newest, largest and most highly rated hotel here; and the new **Hotel Ela** which is close to the slopes. As Borovets is partly a historic rather than a purpose-built resort, there are some hotels a set short bus-ride from the slopes.

A **chalet village**, Malina, has also been built about a mile (2km) from Borovets, linked by a shuttle bus. The chalets have two twin rooms and space for a fifth person in the living room. There is also a **cottage village**, Yagoda, 40 Finnish houses, some with saunas.

THE BALKAN AND CENTRAL REGION

◆◆◆
KOPRIVSHTITSA ✓

The town straddles gentle hills around the Topolnitsa river and its hump-backed bridges. It is on a turning south, towards Strelcha, from the Sofia-Kazanluk-Burgas motorway about 6 miles (10km) beyond Srednogorie.

Its houses attract photographic interest with their flowery courtyards, wooden balconies, bay windows and (sometimes) heavy studded gates. Several of them are museum houses, often linked with people and events

Khisar: people have been taking the waters of its thermal springs for some 7,000 years

in the April Uprising, which can be visited at various times. They are furnished in National Revival style and many have

April Uprising
This tongue-twisting hill town presents a serene picture of Bulgarian National Revival architecture. It is fortuitous that it is so well-preserved, since it was here that the 1876 April Uprising got under way prematurely.

A local patriot shot dead the Turk who came to arrest him on discovering insurrection plans – which included production of cannon from lead-lined cherry trees – then wrote a letter of urgent exhortation to rebels elsewhere, in the blood of the Turk.

interesting artefacts collected by the owners, or small exhibitions.

Every five years, Koprivshtitsa is the setting for a major folklore festival – something the Bulgarians do exceptionally well.

◆◆◆
TROYAN

Troyan, on the road to Kurnare and Sopot from Lovech, is a friendly town where folk enjoy telling you all about themselves, and are perhaps more interesting than the topography. At Oreshak, nearly 4 miles (6km) east, is a folklore school which teaches wood-carving and pottery, and sells craftsware when open to the public in summer.

The high point here is Troyan **Monastery,** founded around 1600, but much of it dating from 1835. The master Zahari Zograph painted the murals inside and outside. Those illustrating Doomsday and Hell are perhaps more suitable for sensitive family viewing than Devilish practices depicted in some ecclesiastical interpretations elsewhere. The church's icons and carvings are by several leading masters. In 1872, Vassil Levski set up a revolutionary committee joined by all the monks and headed by the Father Superior here, making the monastery an early citadel for the 1876 April Uprising.

Accommodation
Hotel Troyan (tel: 0607 24323), unpretentious, overlooking the quaint area by the bridge over the River Osum.

KHISAR (HISSARYA)

Khisar and its hot mineral water springs had attracted long-stay visitors for at least 5,000 years before the Romans came and installed baths, other conveniences and thick brick-and-mortar **defensive walls**. Much of the latter still remain, despite being knocked about by later tourists, including the Crusaders. Their Kamilite Gate is supposed to resemble a camel.

Reached via a turning west after Banya, on the Karlovo–Plovdiv road, the spa provides treatments for digestive, intestinal, gynaecological and arthritic conditions. It also bottles mineral water which is bought all over Bulgaria, recent testimonials having claimed (for instance) total dispersal of kidney stones after drinking it regularly for some months. Visitors drink one of the 22 different waters, at source, from the spouts of teapot-like containers. Roman and later remains offer quite some sightseeing interest.

Accommodation
There are a couple of hotels here to try: the **Balneohotel Augusta**, (tel: 0337 3800), with 540 beds.; or the middle-of-the-road **Apriltse** (tel: 0337 2467). There is also a tourist office in the town.

PLOVDIV
Plovdiv is Bulgaria's second city, but perhaps the one with the most character and variety within itself – even if this is not the first impression from some approaches, or in the

commercial centre.
Its history is many-layered. And
it has a lively present, with its
university, big trade fairs and its
food, tobacco, textile,
metallurgical, machinery, truck-
building, and typewriter-
making industries. Its genuine
period restaurants are better
than most elsewhere in the
country, but its rather
expensive 3-star hotels do not
all provide the sophisticated
level of service and facilities
expected by the international
business community.

*Plovdiv, its old town rich in fine
examples of the National Revival
period houses*

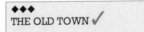

◆◆◆
THE OLD TOWN ✓

Cliché descriptions like quaint
or picturesque hardly do justice
to the elaborately painted
façades, jutting oriel windows,
columns, beams, curving eaves,
and intimate courtyards of the
National Revival Period houses
which rise in serene ceremony
above its cobbled streets.

Mellow and other-wordly as they are, these 18th- to 19th-century preserves are comparatively recent structures on the three hills of ancient *Trimontium*. Here the Romans built a great acropolis with a theatre, whose semi-circle of tiered stone seats, stage and backdrop of classical columns remain sufficiently undamaged by time and tumult to accommodate ambitious drama and music events today. The largest of its kind in Bulgaria, it remains an impressive sight. On the nearby hilltop is a musical academy, and passers-by can hear the voices of vibrant young sopranos or rich-toned basses.

Plovdiv, throughout its long and lively existence, has known many conquerors and invasions. Before the Romans came the Macedonians – in 343BC, when their King Philip II (father of Alexander the Great) seized this hill citadel and called it Philippopolis. But the place had known other names and foundations from the Thracians and early folk for nearly 6,000 years before him. And in various centuries AD the Goths, Byzantines, Bulgarians and Ottomans left their marks – sometimes in more than one period of occupation of this favoured place.

The **modern town** attracts more peaceable influxes from many nations, with its international trade fairs – for consumer goods in May, and technical equipment in September. Discerning business visitors (especially those who benefit from incentive travel schemes)

The Roman theatre, Plovdiv, dating from the 2nd century, where festivals are staged during the summer months

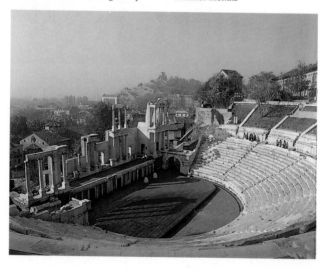

might well find time for the displays at some of Plovdiv's museums (the **Archaeological Museum** has examples of the Panagyurishte 'Thracian Hoard'), and for dining in the genuine period ambience of the Puldin, Alafrangite or Trakiiski Stan restaurants (at the latter International Food and Wine Society members praised the wholesomeness of the food and exceptional quality of vintage and ordinary wines).

In Freedom Park 'Dancing Fountains' are accompanied by music and coloured light effects. Plovdiv Old Town's appeal to artists and writers is obvious. An ochre-tinted edifice on the corner of T Samodumov and K Tsertelov Streets was home in 1833 to the French poet, Lamartine, and contains a small museum of pictures and prose commemorating the house's eminent lodger.

The Georgiadi House has remarkable bay windows and yoke-shaped eaves. At 1 Starinna Street, it houses the **Museum of the National Liberation Struggles** in which the English Lady Strangford is remembered for her philanthropic assistance to the Bulgarians in the 19th century. The **Ethnographic Museum** has ornate gilt wreaths and scrollwork on its bluish-grey façade under a roof which rolls like a sea swell. Its cosily decorated rooms have displays of period furniture, folk items and paintings. In these domestic interiors the atmosphere can perhaps be best appreciated outside the summer tourist season, when

you may be sharing it with polyglot guided tour groups on each echoing floor. There are mosques dating from the mid-15th century – the **Djoumaya** and the **Imaret**. Decorations in the **St Marina Church** on Taxim Tepe Hill include scenes from the life of St George, whose dragon deterrence was well known in these parts. One of Europe's oldest clocktowers is on Sahat Tepe Hill – which also affords a wonderful view.

In Suedinenie (Union) Square is the gleaming modernistic monument to commemorate the 1885 union of Bulgaria with the province of Eastern Rumelia.

Eating Out

Trakiiskistan, Puldin Street (National Revival interior).
Alafrangite, 17 Kiril Nektariev Street.
Puldin, 3 Knyaz Tseretelev Street.
Ribkata, a rare fish tavern (fried carp, trout) in a street parallel with the Central Square as viewed from the front of the Trimontium, known as Patriarch Evtimii.

Accommodation

Hotel Novotel Plovdiv, 5-star, 2 Zlatyu Boyadjiev Street (tel: 034 55892), has international-style modernity in its seven floors, eight suites and 314 double rooms, restaurant, day bar and night club, national restaurant, coffee shop, souvenir shop, indoor and outdoor swimming pools, sauna, bowling alley, hairdressers, post office, covered parking lot, air-conditioning.
Trimontium, 3-star, 2 Kapitan Raicho (tel: 034 225561). Facing

the Central Square, portentously porticoed and vaulted. The Garden Restaurant has Palm Court overtones. It has four floors with four suites and 260 beds, restaurant, night club, national restaurant, coffee shop, hairdressers, post office, information and car rental.

The **Leningrad Park Hotel**, 3-star, 97 Bulgaria Boulevard (tel: 034 55803) is a modern high-rise block in a suburban district. Among its many facilities, it has 21 floors with 26 suites and 675 beds, restaurant, night club, day bar, indoor swimming pool, souvenir shop, hairdresser, post office, coffee shop and information bureau.

Maritsa, Vuzrozhdane Boulevard, 3-star (tel: 034 552735), has 11 floors with four suites, 47 single and 120 double rooms, restaurants, day bar, coffee shop, hairdresser and car rental office.

Bulgaria, 2-star, Patriarh Evtimii Street (tel: 034 26064). This hotel is well situated, in a street parallel to the Central Square.

Leipzig, 2-star, 70 Ruski Boulevard (tel: 034 22501), has 11 floors, two suites and 250 beds, restaurant, night club and information bureau.

KAZANLUK

Kazanluk may be most noted amongst modern Bulgarians for its production of milling machines and musical instruments, but its tourist appeal stems from the fragrant harvest of its **Valley of Roses** – yielding 80 per cent of the world's supply of rose attar for perfumes – and the vivid folklore which follows this.

THE THRACIAN TOMB

A unique attraction in Tyulbeto park on the town's northeastern outskirts. Commemorating a chieftain who was called to higher things around the 4th century BC it features in UNESCO's list of outstanding cultural sites. But its murals, whose 2,300-year-old dyes depict elegant women, soldiers and horses ready for banquet or battle, are sensitive to sunlight and atmosphere, so the public sees a detailed replica built near the original tomb. The original is opened up only occasionally for the specialist archaeologist or VIP.

MUSEUM OF THE ROSE INDUSTRY

Illustrates the history of this business since its first blooming 150 or more years ago, with ancient sepia photographs, huge distilling kettles, and examples of the rose oil's use in 'green' medicines, rose liqueur, and various confections. And the Rose Institute has collected more than 1,500 rose species from all over the world.

FESTIVAL OF THE VALLEY OF THE ROSES

This takes place over several days in late May or early June between a nearby Balkan Valley and the main square of other-wise ordinary-looking Kazanluk (best to check exact dates with the Bulgarian National Tourist Office or Balkantourist, coach tours take in Kazanluk and the Valley). Be sure to plan a visit to this lovely event if you are in

Gathering rosebuds during May (and June): rose-pickers in folk costume celebrate the annual Festival of Roses

Bulgaria at this time.
For some time, pickers in prettily embroidered folk garb will daily have been gathering rosebuds while they may – from pre-dawn until 08.00, or whenever the morning sun becomes so hot as to steam away the precious aroma from the dewy petals of pink *rosa damascena* or white *rose alba*. The 'rose maidens' empty basketfuls of blossoms into quaint mule-carts for despatch, in procession, to town and distillery. They are welcomed with a confetti of rose petals and a liberal spraying with rosewater (a dilution of the attar, which is literally worth its weight in gold).
Tape recorders pick up fluttering cadences from rustic flute, oriental fiddle and Balkan bagpipe, and great cowbells strike an awesome, pagan note when hung around the torsos of evil-spirit-scaring 'demons' wearing head-masks.
The annual Rose Festival's folk extravaganza has been known to enchant even tourists who would normally switch off at the threat of folklore. Gorgeously costumed, the dancers and singers are the best from each of their regions.

Accommodation
Hotel Kazanluk, 3-star (tel: 0431 27210), with amenities including indoor swimming pool, restaurants, bars and a *Mehana* tavern selling snacks and excellent draught beer.
Hotel Roza, 2-star (tel: 0431 24703).
Hotel Zornitsa, 2-star (tel 0431 20084).
These are all in the centre of town, and there is a **campsite** about 3 miles (5km) along the Shipka road, reached very cheaply by bus.

Balkantourist Office at the Hotel Kazanluk.

♦♦♦
ETURA ✓

Etura, an open-air museum park where craftsmen work in traditional workshops making individual souvenirs

Etura Ethnographical Museum, 5 miles (8km) from Gabrovo, is much cosier than its name may suggest. It is an artistic reproduction, with authentic atmosphere, of a village street with traditional workshops, in a lovely wooded valley by a stream which drives a watermill. The houses, workrooms and shops are simply but attractively built, sometimes of stone with weather-boarding and a little wooden balcony; carved shutters, under overhanging eaves of heavy shingled roofs. Their interiors tend to smell of wood and whatever material is being hand-worked by the resident craftspeople – leather for old-style wine containers or harnesses, sheep's wool for spinning and weaving into rugs, cloth for items of folkwear, the paraphernalia of metalworkers, potters, painters and musical instrument makers. (Craft courses can be arranged for visitors, by arrangement through the tourist office.) Here you can buy souvenirs, including silver, gold and copperware, all with more individual character than the mass-produced offerings of the more commercialised shops in resort areas. You may also be tempted by the aroma of fresh 'organic' bread and buns from the bakery, or the sizzle of meaty sausages at a tavern. Some of the crafts shops may be closed on certain days, perhaps with a frustrating lack of information as to when they will open. But there is a refreshing absence of commercial hassle.

SHIPKA PASS

This is one of the places where Bulgaria's friendship with Russia can be seen to be deeply forged. It saw one of the most decisive battles of the three-prong Russian military incursion to drive out the cruelly dominant Turks in the hard winter of 1877.
Here 7,000 besieged Russian soldiers and Bulgarian volunteers kept at bay 27,000 élite troops of Suleiman Pasha, finally beating them off – and advancing rapidly southwards towards the Turkish border when the Russians sent reinforcements after taking Pleven in another key struggle. When their ammunition ran out after days of stubborn defence, they had hurled rocks, tree boughs and corpses at the Turks.

SHIPKA MEMORIAL CHURCH

On the wooded hillside above Shipka village, this commemorates the battle at Shipka Pass. The church has 17 bells, 12 of which were cast entirely from melted-down shell-cases and shrapnel found on the battlefield. Today, visiting Bulgarians and Russians of all ages place flowers and wreaths by the memorial tablets in the church's crypt.

FREEDOM MONUMENT

On nearby Stoletov Peak. Having climbed the steps to the monument, visitors can descend to slake thirsts or eat at cafés in a parking area below – cafés whose facilities do *not* share the epic quality of the monuments.
Bulgaria's most famous yoghurt, made with buffalo milk, can be sampled here.

GABROVO

Gabrovo overturns stereotype preconceptions about stone-faced or unimaginative bureaucracy in this part of the world – the town's **House of Humour and Satire** is the headquarters for local, national and imported items of humour, such as carnival masks, witty writings, silly sketches, clown costumes and other artefacts designed to make you laugh. The house itself has cool white marble interiors with the rather clinical look, as it were, of a modern art gallery.
Gabrovo's occasional Experimental Satirical Theatre performances are apparently broadly based programmes of

comedy, music and carnivalia at its Biennial Festival of Humour and Satire, staged in May each odd-numbered year. A description of Gabrovo as 'one of Bulgaria's prettiest towns' seems somewhat prone to poetic licence or local humour, since it does not have such obvious eye-appeal as have Plovdiv Old Town, Koprivshtitsa, Nesebur, Sozopol and numerous other places. Its more tangible and serious products come from textile mills, machine shops, and 'the world's biggest combine for building electric hoists'. It has

The golden-domed church in Shipka, built in memory of those who fell in the fiercest battle of the Russo-Turkish war

many technical colleges. There are atmospheric, older enclaves flanking the River Yantra, in which a rock supports the stature of the town's 14th-century founder, Raicho the Blacksmith. And tradition is handed down in crafts shops, some of them along Opulchenska Street.
The **National Museum of Education** is housed in the Aprilov school, set up in 1835 as the first school to provide secular teaching in the Bulgarian language.
In the town's main square, there is a memorial to Mitko Palaouzov – a 14-year-old partisan who died fighting Fascists in 1944.

Eating Out
The Inn, 15 Opulchenska Street, a fairly folksy national taverna – as is the **Mogilyov** on Plaza Purvi Mai.

Accommodation
Hotel Balkan, 3-star, 14 Emanouil Manolov Street (tel: 066 21911), with three banqueting halls, coffee shop, day bar.
Yantra, 2-star, Railway Station Square (tel: 066 24812), with restaurant and bar. **Campsites:** there are two campsites here, the **Ljubovo** is southeast of town, and the **Hemus** is to the northeast.

Balkantourist Office 2 Opulchenska Street (tel: 066 24831).

BOZHENTSI
Bozhentsi, a village which rambles around its rural valley as randomly as do the roses in

its sometimes overgrown gardens, is a special architectural and historic preserve.

Charming, indeed, are the woodcarvings on the entrance gates and verandahs of its whitewashed houses along cobblestone streets. But they do not now echo with the sounds of old-fashioned artisan labour. One or two former dwellings are museum-houses which can be visited by coach tour parties, their intentions having 19th-century folk-furnishings. For the average visitor, Bozhentsi offers pleasant and very peaceful sightseeing walks – but not much indigenous life.

◆◆◆ VELIKO TURNOVO ✓

More wholly picturesque and preserved than some ancient cities, Veliko Turnovo presents a splendid theatrical backdrop to its history since (and before) it was fortress capital of the Second Bulgarian State from 1187 to 1396.

It seems to grow naturally out of the rock of three hills above several loops of the River Yantra. In almost Disneyesque (but dignified) jumbles, its older dwellings – sturdily beamed and tiled, sometimes balconies, hung with creepers and roses – terrace its contours or cling to cliff-edges like elaborate nests of martins under house-eaves. It was on Tsarevets Hill that, in 1185, the brothers Assen and Peter seized the fortress and led an uprising which eventually freed Bulgaria from

Byzantine rule. Its ramparts, gates and battle towers are often spotlit at night; within the walls archaeologists have for years excavated the remains of the royal palace, religious and mercantile buildings.

On Tsarevets and Trapezitsa Hills, antiquities include surviving churches that are rich in murals and monuments – notably those of St Dimiter of Salonika (12th-century), the Holy Forty Martyrs (13th-century) and St Peter and Paul (14th-century).

On Sveta Gora Hill was a medieval monastery with schools of literature and painting which produced masterpieces like Tsar Ivan Alexander's *Four Gospels* (in the British Museum, London) and the Manasses' *Chronicle* (in the Vatican Library, Rome).

Now its supports the city's Cyril and Methodius University – named after the 9th-century monks who devised the original Cyrillic script of Slav languages. Many of the buildings which give the city its distinctive character today date from the National Revival Period of the 18th and 19th centuries. Numerous examples are by self-taught architect Kolyo Ficheto, 'founder' of the Bulgarian national style of architecture, which conforms with the landscape and combines new features with medieval traditions. Especially worth seeing are the House with the Monkey, at 14 Vustanicheska Street, the Hadji Nikoli Inn, 17 Rakovski Street, the Town Hall in Suedinenie Square, and the Samovodene Market Place, with

Veliko Turnovo: memorial to the brothers Assen and Peter who led the 1185 uprising against Byzantine rule

its restored workshops, café and exhibition section.

The **archaeological museum**, dealing with Veliko Turnovo's 12th to14th-century period as capital of Bulgaria, is at 21 Boteva Street.

Four miles (7km) northwest of the city, on a secluded hillside, is **Preobrazhenski Monastery** (open to the public), former safe refuge of the revolutionary Vassil Levski. Prepare for the monastery to be shrouded in scaffolding or even closed to visitors, as it suffered serous storm damage in 1991 and renovations may be still in progress.

Eating Out
Slavyatrka restaurant, café and night club, 35 Levski Street.
Stadion restaurant, 2 T Balina Street.
Vladishki Most tavern, Assenovo suburb.
Poltava café, 1 Hristo Botov Street.
Oriental café, 32 D Blagoev Street.

Accommodation
Interhotel Veliko Turnovo, 3-star, 2 E Popov Street (tel: 062

30571). Amenities include disco.

Yantra Hotel, 2-star, 1 Velchova Zavera Square (tel: 062 20391).

Etur Hotel, 2-star, 1 Ivailo Street (tel: 062 26851).

Balkantourist Office, 1 V Levski Street (tel: 062 21836).

◆◆
ARBANASSI

Secluded on high ground just north of Veliko Turnovo, Arbanassi is one of Bulgaria's most attractive and unusual villages. Its stone-built houses are decorated externally with floral and geometrical figures carved or figured with large-headed nails in wood panelling, doors and shutters. Carved wooden ceilings are popular, and often feature 'sunburst' designs. In the 17th and 18th centuries, craftsmen in copper, gold and silverware flourished here. In early spring they would set off on merchant venturer trips, their caravans stocked with hides, dried meat, sausage, wool, furs and wine. They travelled to Hungary, Italy, Poland, Russia, even Persia and India, returning with silks, velvet and spices.

There are two monasteries, the **St Nikola**, whose chapel's filigree work is particularly beautiful and intricate – and the **Holy Virgin**. Each of the five village churches has an eastern section traditionally intended for men and a western (rear) section for women. The stark-looking exterior of the **Holy Nativity (Rozhdestvo Hristovo) Church** belies the exceptional wealth of painted murals within.

SHUMEN (SHOUMEN)

Shumen is one of the Bulgarian names seen on bottles of its district's exported white wine, as well as of beer locally. An industrially important town, roughly halfway between Veliko Turnovo and Varna, it has character, culture – and vintage history.

Preslav

Located just south of Shumen, Preslav was the second capital (succeeding Pliska) of the First Bulgarian Kingdom under Tsar Simeon around the turn of the 9th/10th century, and it was from its famous academic institutions that the Slav alphabet was spread to other countries. Unfortunately, various medieval occupiers were less culturally inclined than Simeon, having tendencies to raze the city to the ground or burn it down. Thus, much that remains of the original site of Veliki (Great) Preslav is marked out by ruined columns. However, there has been considerable restoration of the castle walls, palace buildings – and the Round Church, which is a unique example of Old Bulgarian architecture.

In recent years, excavators have unearthed sections of the archbishop's building, the basilica, the city wall and a decorated pool. And the Veliki Preslav Museum in the archaeological reserve contains rare antiquities from the 10th century.

Just east of Preslav is the Patleina Monastery.

In the traditional style: heavy tiled roof, broad eaves, wide balcony, white-washed walls

The **Historical Museum** on Slavyanski Boulevard, and the **Lajos Kossuth Museum**, 35 Tsar Osvoboditel Street, are interesting.
The town's older quarters are down by the river. Its symphony orchestra is Bulgaria's oldest; there is opera and theatre. During the First and Second Bulgarian States, and later, it was a key fortress. The fort's foundations are Roman and Thracian.

◆◆
1,300 YEARS OF BULGARIA MEMORIAL
A massive concatenation of concrete figures on Ilchov Bair Hill.

◆
THE TOMBUL MOSQUE
Built in 1745 with materials from

the ancient local towns, the largest in the country. An erstwhile museum, this is once again a working mosque, and as such may be closed to visitors at certain times.

Accommodation
Hotel Madara, 3-star (tel: 054 57598), in the town centre, with restaurant, coffee-shop, tavern, tourist information and car rental offices.
Hotel Sofia (moderately priced), 37 Tsar Osboditel Street. Bookings through Balkantourist office (see below).

Balkantourist Office Rakovski Street (tel: 054 55313).
Car repairs: 14 Gagarin Street.
Union of Bulgarian Motorists office: 1 Tsvetan Zangov Street.

◆◆◆
MADARA
The Madara National Historical and Archaeological Reserve, near the village of Madara 6

miles (10km) east of Shumen, contains the famous bas-relief of the **Madara Horseman** cut into the rock of an ancient cliff fortress.

Inscriptions below him, though in Greek, date from the reign of Khan Omurtag (816-31) and refer to 8th- and 9th-century events in Bulgaria. Others have suggested he may have appeared much earlier than that, and with a religious significance.

Holding a goblet in one hand, he sits astride a proud-stepping steed, with a hound pursuivant and speared lion couchant on the ground below him.

On a terrace below are remains of a 9th-century pagan shrine and ecclesiastical buildings from the late Middle Ages. To the southwest are ruins of Roman houses and farm buildings.

PLISKA

Pliska is more than the name of a popular Bulgarian brandy. It was the first capital of Bulgaria, from the 7th century until Preslav supplanted it in 893. Unlike the village which bears its name today, the ancient city of Pliska was grand and powerful.

FORTIFICATION RUINS

Ruins of three concentric fortifications, covering 9 square miles (23 sq km), 2 miles (1.2km) from the village which is on a turning north from Kaspichan on E70 (east of Shumen).

The best preserved remains are of the Great Palace, but other remnants include those of a small palace with water mains that were previously unknown, and of the Great Basilica from the 9th century. The nearby museum contains pottery, weapons and other items from a site which may engage archaeologists for some time to come.

KOTEL

A characterful town with traditional carpet, rug and blanket-making industries, Kotel lies in a hollow of hill country on a road north towards Omurtag from E772, 19 miles (31km) east of Sliven.

It was the home of several Bulgarian National Revival Period revolutionaries and writers including Georgi Rakovski and Sophronius. There are schools for folk-instrument making and for arts and crafts, at which Balkantourist may arrange courses for visitors (with advance notice).

Kotel carpets have geometric patterns in strong colours. Both they and the tufted or fleecy rugs find a ready export market. Along narrow cobblestone streets of the **old part of the town**, which survived a great fire of 1894, are wood-clad houses with good carvings and broad eaves. An **Ethnographic Museum** is in one of them, and not far away (these things are not done by halves!) is the **History Museum** in an old school building.

Accommodation

The **Hotel Kotel**, 2-star (tel: 0453 2865), has restaurant and discothèque.

◆◆
ZHERAVNA

This is a pretty 'living museum' village, 9 miles (14km) along a turning to the west, south of Kotel. Houses of the 18th and 19th centuries have been restored to their original appearance, with their rounded roof tops, jutting eaves and oriel windows, and wood carvings. Modern fittings have been installed without disturbing the character of their interiors – furnished with divans, traditional carpets, rugs, curtains and runners.

A bakery and church café have also been resurrected and put back into business. Craftsmen's shops and a tavern with restaurant have been added, in architecture which is intended to harmonise.

The former houses of Russ Chorbadzhi, Sava Filaretov, and Dimcho Kehaya are said to be

Monument to National Revival notable, Sophronius, in Kotel, his native town

museum pieces especially worth seeing.

SLIVEN

This is an important industrial town on the southeast edge of the Balkan range, at the foot of the **Sinite Kamani ('Blue Rocks') mountain**. Several museums have memorabilia of revolutionary action against the Turks and others, but textiles are mainly what the town turns out today. In the **Historical Museum**, in the main street, are housed artefacts from the grave of a Thracian chieftain buried in the locality with Maingly, his best horse.

Accommodation

The Hotel Sliven, 2-star (tel: 044 27065), in the centre of town, has a restaurant, bar, discothèque, café, and Balkantourist office.
The Zora, 1-star, 1 Mitropolit Seraphim Street.
Bookings may be made through the Balkantourist office.

THE RHODOPES AND THE SOUTH

PAMPOROVO

For the skier Pamporovo starts with two great advantages. The Rhodope mountains in which it lies stretch along the Greek border about 53 miles (85km) from Plovdiv and catch the moisture in the winds as they blow up from the Aegean. In winter this falls as snow and gives a long and quite snow-sure season. The second advantage is the sun. At a latitude further south than that of Rome, Pamporovo enjoys hot sunshine.

Another Greek connection is Orpheus, who according to legend was born near

Pamporovo, an international ski centre, is also a popular mountain resort in summer

Pamporovo and now has a hotel named after him. There is still plenty of music in the restaurants and discos – often live groups playing ancient-looking instruments – and dancing and singing to traditional airs forms part of the entertainment.
The skiing is of good intermediate standard with six main lifts covering an area between the village at 5,250 feet (1,600m) and the top of Snezhanka at 6,319 feet (1,962m). At this point there is a radio beacon with a revolving restaurant, which gives spectacular views over the

surrounding countryside.
As the skiing is mostly on north-facing slopes, the snow escapes the sun and remains powdery. The runs are cut through quite dense forest and provide variety. There are easy blues, some longish reds and short sharp black slopes so that beginners, intermediates and experts can all enjoy the challenge. It is not too big an area – about right for an intermediate skier over a week's holiday.

It is also an excellent resort for beginners. The 60-man Bulgarian ski school is well organised; classes rarely exceed 12 and the instructors are competent in foreign languages.

A great many schools organise skiing trips to Pamporovo and

much of the accommodation, therefore, is economical, consisting of bunks in rooms with showers, in hotels serving nourishing but basic food. There are, however, good three-star hotels and the fact that the school operators send large numbers to the resort means that they get excellent rates for adults too, even when the accommodation and food is of a much higher standard. The **Perelik Hotel**, for example, has an indoor swimming pool, sauna, gymnasium, bowling alley and a good selection of shops including **Corecom**. Its rates for half board in a twin-bedded room are about half those for a comparable Swiss hotel.

In the evening there are the usual entertainments – sleighrides, barbecues with whole lambs spit-roasted on open fires, taverns and discos to

The Rhodope Mountains and southern Bulgaria

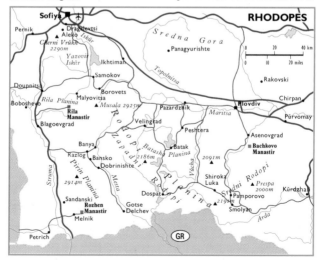

Picturesque Shiroka Luka: traditional houses perch on the mountain slopes above the main village street

use up any energy left after a day on the slopes. Among the other hotels in Pamporovo are the **Mourgavets**, with snooker club, the **Rozhen**, with new karioki bar and the **Panorama**, with a good view. All the incidentals to a holiday – ski hire, the odd meal, a cup of coffee – are less expensive in Bulgaria than in the Alps. It is also a good place to buy presents. Bulgarians make good carved wooden toys and ornaments in the mountains and their Pliska brandy is cheap and potent. Many presents are worth buying in the ski resorts.

In some Eastern bloc countries equipment hire can be a gamble but Bulgaria imports good quality skis, bindings and boots. The hire shop takes care that the bindings suit the weight and ability of the skier and boots are fitted carefully so that no sore heels or squashed feet take the pleasure out of skiing. Altogether Pamporovo is a good place to start skiing – the patient ski-school, easy slopes and low prices combine with the southern sunshine to provide an excellent holiday.

◆◆◆
SHIROKA LUKA
This little village has a medieval, fairytale appearance, enchanting and authentic. It is a typical, but superb example of

a traditional Rhodopean mountain village, and an easy trip from Pampovoro. It can be reached on the road down from there (or from Smolyan) to Devin, at a point where tall mountain pines begin to merge with varieties of broad-leaved trees and there are clearings with tiny cow pastures. The main street is as quaint as the steep little lanes where weatherboarded houses and barns cling to the mountain rock. And here the keen photographer may regret not having brought in more film – hard to find, even in Pamporovo, although there are Kodak concession shops in most resorts now.

On the terraces of a tavern or two, you can sit on a half-log bench at a half-tree-trunk table and listen to birdsong.

SCHOOL OF FOLK MUSIC

If you arrive with a tour group, there may be a pre-arranged concert by pupils, aged 13 to 19, who will have competed nationwide for places at the School of Folk Music on the southern side of this village. With a variety of plucked or bowed instruments, or a kaval flute, or a bagpipe, they can play or sing in numerous widely differing regional styles and cadences.

Perhaps they may intone 'The Haidouk Came Out...' the typical Rhodopean song taped by Valia Balkanska. (This was chosen to accompany tapes of Beethoven's 'Ode to Joy' and other Earth-representative themes aboard the American

spacecraft *Voyager*, in case it is ever intercepted by some intelligence beyond our solar system.)

They learn to make instruments, including bagpipes. And there are special days when Shiroka Luka shrills with the sound of a hundred pipers gathered from the Bulgar highlands far and wide – though perhaps only every other year.

SMOLYAN

Smolyan, 62 miles (100km) south of Plovdiv and 3,310 feet (1,010m) up in the Rhodopes, has 'a climate that is particularly

Bachkovo Monastery, artistically one of the country's most significant sites

To the east is the Oustovo section, one of the original villages, which also has some striking National Revival houses. There are buses to **Smolyan Lakes** amidst high pastures north of the town, which offer trout fishing and craggy scenery with forests that may contain deer and bears.

◆◆
MUSEUM and ART GALLERY
Two of the town's special amenities are especially worth a visit.

Accommodation
Hotels include the **Smolyan**, 3-star (tel: 0301 23293), whose extensive main restaurant overlooks the Cherna river's wooded valley. The hotel has Balkantourist and car rental offices. In the skiing season (particularly), bus services connect it daily with Pamporovo.
Panorama campsite, 2-star.

Union of Bulgarian Motorists
Deveti Septemvri Street, Raikovo section.

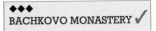

◆◆◆
BACHKOVO MONASTERY ✓

The oldest monastery in Bulgaria, Bachkovo Monastery (Bachkovo Manastir) is about 43 miles (70km) north of Smolyan towards Plovdiv, and 5 miles (9km) south of Asenovgrad – which produces the famous full-bodied red Mavrud wine for home and overseas consumption.
Just above Bachkovo village, with chickens pecking amongst its courtyard cobbles, the

beneficial for the vocalist'. It has organised summer opera singing courses in a newly built local theatre, and singing is an activity in which Bulgarian experts are in a super-class of their own.
It has flourished remarkably since 1960, when it was rebuilt and combined with two other villages which had once been ruined by the Turks because their people would not convert to Islam under pain of death.

monastery has a more 'domestic' atmosphere than some others. Some of its murals, however, do depict nasty things happening to sinners in Hell, who happen to resemble 19th-century notables of Plovdiv who refused to open a Bulgarian school in the city. The artist is Zahari Zograph, the most famous National Revival artist, who permits himself a self-portrait in better company. There are other notable paintings in the refectory. The monastery was founded in 1083, originally for Georgian monks. The architecture of the one remaining building of this period contains elements of Armenian, Georgian and Syrian building styles in rows of stone and brick.

BATAK

This is the place where Turkish atrocities became so barbaric in 1876 as finally to shock the world into recognition that something must be done, thanks to the uncensored reporting of a brave American journalist.

◆◆
ST NEDELYA'S CHURCH

To suppress local activities following the April Uprising, the Turks and their Pomak henchmen besieged 3,000 citizens in the church and then – after promising immunity for surrender – proceeded mercilessly to behead and butcher virtually every man, woman and child in the church and its yard. Blood-stained palm-prints remain on the church walls.

European reaction to these atrocities was not entirely decisive. In Britain, for instance, Disraeli wanted a continued alliance with the Turks against the Russians, although this met with strong opposition from others.

Despite this history, detailed in the church and a local museum, Batak and its surroundings – with beech and pine forests, and carp-fishing in the dam are regarded as a peaceful recreation area. It is 27 miles (37km) south of the E80 from Pazardzhik.

Accommodation

The youth tourist organisation **Orbita** (tel: 2327) has local hostel accommodation.

VELINGRAD

Named after a partisan heroine, Vela Peeva, and developed from three merged villages in 1948, Velingrad is a leafy spa with parkland, 77 warm mineral water springs and 40 balneo-therapy establishments treating various conditions from rheumatoid arthritis to hypertension and nervous fatigue. There is a 'Holiday Palace' of the trade unions. Velingrad is 10 miles (16km) east of Yundola resort, which is 16 miles (26km) south of Belovo (E80).

Eating Out

The **Kleptouza Restaurant** overlooks the Kleptouza karst lake, in the Chepino Quarter, which sometimes has rowing boats.

Accommodation

The **Zdravets Hotel**, 2-star (tel: 0359 2682), caters inexpensively for westerners, as may local campsites and chalets.

THE BLACK SEA

CAPE KALIAKRA

This is a scenic promontory 7 miles (12km) east of Kavarna in the north of Bulgaria's Black Sea coastline. Its cliffs rear up more than 200 feet (60m), and from them 40 Bulgarian maidens are said to have thrown themselves into the sea rather than face a fate worse than death from Ottomans.

There are caves which contain an archaeological museum and a restaurant.

BALCHIK

Founded in the 6th century BC Balchik, 5 miles (8km) north of Albena, looks, in part, more like a traditional seaside resort than any.

The local mineral waters are recommended for gastro-intestinal upsets.

◆◆◆
BOTANICAL GARDEN

Straddling several cliff terraces, this contains 3,000 species of plants from numerous countries. It was the park of the small former palace of Queen Maria of Romania, built in Oriental style, with minaret, in 1924. (This area was owned by Romania between 1913 and 1940.) Ancient amphorae and tombstones are amongst the park's curiosities, which also include a church transferred piecemeal from a Greek island.

Eating Out
Restaurant Dionysopolis, with bar.

Accommodation
Hotel Balchik, 2-star (tel: 0579 2175), 68 beds, with restaurant.

The Stone Forest, a weird natural phenomenon near Varna

Hotel Raketa, 1-star (tel: 0579 2175), 36 beds.
Campsite Bisser, 1 mile (2km) south.

Balkantourist Office 33 Georgi Dimitrov Street (tel: 0579 3448)

ALBENA

Not to be confused with Albania (by contrast with whose attitudes to fun and frolic this might seem in spirit to be the Malibu Beach scene), Albena is named after a beautiful girl in a well known story by Yordan Yovkov.

'For the Young at Heart' is its promotional tag, and it is the youngest major resort chronologically. Along the 4-mile (7km) powdery sand beach of its bay, backed by hills, its hotels are sometimes in 'pyramid' architecture not unlike that at La Grande Motte in France's Languodoc-Roussillon. It is about 6 miles (10km) north of Golden Sands. The seabed shelves very

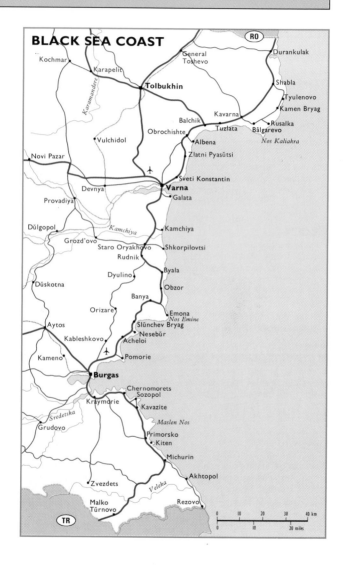

BLACK SEA COAST

gradually, so that the average adult is about shoulder-deep at 165 yards (150m) off shore. Sports and recreational facilities are similar in scope to those at Golden Sands (pages 70–71) and Sunny Beach (pages 77 and 79) and those for the youngest visitors (see **Children**, pages 107-109).

At the **Kamelia Hotel Club**, children of Balkan Holiday clients enjoy special programmes of amusement, including disco.

The big **Dobruja Hotel** has an olympic-size swimming pool with mineral water, a balneo-therapy department, and conference halls with simultaneous translation facilities. It is open year-round. The **Orehite Picnic**, up in a walnut tree forest, is a restaurant whose folklore includes something very rare and genuine – '**fire-walking**' and barefoot dancing on glowing embers amidst whiffs of woodsmoke and a strange, almost pagan atmosphere. The **Slavyanska Kut Restaurant** features dances of the various Slav peoples, though not on anything red-hot.

Kamchiya, near Varna, a resort set in a nature reserve

THE BLACK SEA

The Cultural Information Centre provides diversions from Happy Birthday parties with zodiacal themes to Evenings of Bulgarian Humour, which may or may not lose something in translation if it is as thorough as Bulgarians like to be in some matters.

Excursions
Balchik; Cape Kaliakra; Nesebur, by hydrofoil or by horse-and-cart (two days) through the leafy, fertile Dobruja countryside.

Accommodation
Reservations can be made through the Albena Booking Office, tel: 05722 2063/2920.

GOLDEN SANDS
(Zlatni Pyasutsi)
Though its Anglicized name may sound kitsch, Golden Sands and its setting of lush forested hills and adjacent low cliffs 10 miles (17km) north of Varna have attracted more cheers than sneers from foreign pundits. 'Nowhere else in Europe have I seen such a splendid architectural ensemble, blending so perfectly with nature', enthused Jean Royer, director of the School of Architecture in Paris. Golden Sands has a Cultural Information Centre. And its nightlife has touches of glamour which might betoken 'high living' expenses elsewhere. Its Hotel International is among several which open year-round. The resort's visitors are international, with a predominence of British and German tourists. Refurbishment has been visited on numerous early-1960s hotels which were fraying at the edges, and the general scene appears somewhat upmarket of bigger but otherwise largely similar Sunny Beach (see page 77) (though updating has been carried out there, too).

Though less extensive than Sunny Beach's, the clean golden sands are 2.5 miles (4km) long and up to 30 feet (100m) wide. Beach umbrellas, chairs and pedalos can be hired cheaply, and in three areas there are changing

Sozopol, a picturesque old town with several beaches in the area

rooms with mineral-water showers and first-aid booths. Yachts can be hired through Balkantourist; also dinghies, motorboats, water skis, wind-surfing boards, and sub-aqua gear – with expert tuition for each, as needed.

The sea is warm and normally calm, though there are efficient lifeguard precautions. Children can enjoy a wide range of diversions, and can have their own menus in most restaurants (see **Children** pages 107-109). The Luna Park, near the Rodina Hotel, provides gentle lunacy for most age groups. It has ways of making you laugh with distorting mirrors, shriek on the 60-foot (18m) high slalom dry slide and its four 160-foot (50m) chutes, shoot in the electronic shooting range, contemplate in the cosmodrome or at the giant chess board.

There's even talk of cricket near the Malina Hotel, which also offers archery and mini-golf. Bulgaria hasn't noticeably gone in for proper golf yet, although this might help increase its international conference and incentive-travel business.

Horsemanship has been quite a native skill since Thracian and Khanate times, and the riding ground 220 yards (200m) south of the Republika bus stop) has expert instructors. Resort roads are very safe, and bicycles or rickshaw-trikes can be hired near the Malina, Liliya and Rodina hotels. The Kamchia Hotel offers pin-bowling and video games.

Entertainment

Numerous hotels provide evening entertainment with various types of dancing. Discothèques are at the Astoria, Gdansk, Pliska and Veliko Turnovo hotels. And there are two open-air ones: the Kolibi, which probably scares the nightingales in surrounding woodland, and the hillside Koukeri.

Folklore crops up in at least 15 restaurants. Even ultra-sophisticates who wince at this word may find folklore in Bulgaria to be more exciting, and often a more genuine living tradition, than in some other holiday countries.

Preserved through the centuries of oppression: Nesebur has a number of fine old churches

The menu and programme at the Kosharata aims 'to acquaint visitors with the lifestyle of the Bulgarian shepherds'. Yes, you do see such folk with their flocks out in the countryside. Shepherds do play their flutes and whittle designs on sticks; shepherdesses do spin wool with hand-spindles.
Bulgarians sometimes tend to suspect some gypsies of laziness and smuggling interests. But the silk-costumed real gypsies at the Tsiganski Tabor tented 'gypsy camp' exceed norms of virtuosity and vivacity in song and dance, while their audience can lounge in 'gypsy carts' drinking good Bulgarian 'champagne'.

Shopping
Shopping Centre, near the post office: ceramics, wood and copper, home-spun weaves, embroidery. Perfumery and cosmetics, knitwear, ready-wear, footwear, beach articles and sports gear.
Gladiola shop, at the Gladiola Hotel: ready-wear knitwear, leather wear, carpets.
Kriva Lipa bazaar, knitwear, ready-wear, perfumery, souvenirs.

Nympha bazaar, on the south beach: beach articles, ceramics, perfumery, souvenirs.
Trifon Zarezan bazaar, next to Trifon Zarezan restaurant: knitwear, haberdashery, jewellery, perfumery.
Bowling shop, souvenirs, perfumery, jewellery.
Troyan Shop, opposite the Havana pool: wood and copper souvenirs, ceramics, homespun weaves, embroidery.
Souvenir palace, opposite the Stariya Dub restaurant: beach articles, leather wear, souvenirs, drinks.
Morsko Oko bazaar, next to the Morsko Oko Hotel: perfumery, cosmetics, souvenirs, drinks.
Representative store of the Union of Bulgarian Artists, opposite the Zlatna Kotva Hotel: original applied art work, leather wear, embroidery, ceramics, wood and copper souvenirs.
Company Store of the SI Peev Glass Factory, at the Rodina Hotel: glassware and ceramics.
Book and record selling pavilions, opposite the Mimoza and Rodina hotels.
For reduced-cost western jewellery, perfumery, cosmetics, ready-wear, cigarettes and drinks, there are several **Corecom** shops at the Shopping Centre in the International, Shipka, Ambassador and Astoria hotels, and in the Nympha, Kaliakra and Morsko Oko stores.

Eating Out
The **Vodenitsata**, up in the hills, is a convincing reproduction of an old water-mill, and its meaty menu includes a rich sausage-and-lentil soup. Fish and seafood fans find more limited scope locally, though the **Zlatna Ribka** at the beach's northern end specialises in this – on its sun terrace or indoors.

Accommodation
Hotel reservations may be made through the Golden Sands and Sveti Konstantin Booking Office, tel: 052 855681. See also Tourist Service Offices, below.

Tourist Service Offices
For information, currency exchange, excursions, entertainment, accommodation bookings, etc: near the Casino restaurant; at the International Hotel; at Trifon Zarezan restaurant; at the Cultural Centre; at the Kriva Lipa bazaar; at the Ambassador, Briz, Zlatna Kotva, Kristal, Morsko Oko, Preslav and Shipka Hotels, as well as at the Panorama campsite.

SVETI KONSTANTIN (DRUZHBA)
Sveti Konstantin, is the longest-established post-war resort, with a tranquil and intimate ambience. About 6 miles (10km) north of Varna along E87, which gives aspects of a bosky riviera, it is graced by stately old oaks, beech, poplars, pine, cedar, cypress and lime trees. In July and August there are folk concerts. Holiday homes restore the tissues of the resort's visitors, who can take the local mineral waters. Little rocky coves and beaches combine with an

overall smallness of scale to provide contrast to the three large coastal resorts (Sunny Beach, Golden Sands and Albena). There is a frequent bus service to Varna and Golden Sands.

Eating Out

The **Odessos Restaurant** and the folkloric **Bulgarian Wedding** restaurant are both near the hotels listed below. Other restaurants: **Manastirska Izba** (Monastery Cellar), **The Sedemte Odai** (The Seven Chambers) and **Taverna Chernomorets** (Black Sea) taverna with its Tourist Service Bureau.

Accommodation

The Grand Hotel Varna, 5-star (tel: 052 61491), big, and one of the finest on the coast. Its facilities include tennis courts, bowling alley, and sauna and a variety of health treatments in its balneological complex. For all of these attractions charges are made in *sterling* (such extra charges are not uncommon). Guests can, however, enjoy free use of both the hotel's outdoor mineral-water swimming pool and indoor sea-water pool (both heated), a nightclub with cabaret and a casino.
Of the 20 hotels, this is one of those used by European tour operators. Others include: **The Prostor**, 2-star (tel: 052 61171), 50 yards (45m) from the beach and of 1950s vintage, its terrace having an attractive use of stone (plentiful in Bulgaria, but international-style concrete and glass is the coastal norm).
The seven-storey beach-front **Rubin** (with its Tourist Service Bureau), 2-star (tel: 052 61020). The low-rise **Koral**, 2-star (tel: 052 61414).
Reservations can also be made through the Golden Sands and Sveti Konstantin Booking Office (tel: 052 855681/861301).

VARNA

This is Bulgaria's third city and a major seaport, with a long history and a multi-cultural present. It retains Roman and other remains, exudes a friendly atmosphere in ornamented late 19th-century avenues and public buildings, and has added modern developments in human scale and leafy settings.
It is popular with package tourists who fly into its airport to stay in surrounding resorts, both from foreign countries and Bulgaria itself, sports champions, and world professional bodies attending congresses (sociologists and architects have been among them).
It has serious everyday business in shipbuilding, power generation, the food and light industries; its major university institutes of Economics, Electrical Engineering and Medicine, and its Naval Academy. Early evening seems to bring out a relaxed, Mediterranean-style 'promenading' custom in summer.
The Varna Summer Festival in June or July presents theatre performances in the former Roman thermal baths, chamber music amidst the icons of the old St Atanas Church, the ballet contest on the open air stage,

and symphony concerts at the Festival Complex. This latter, on the corner of Slivnitsa and Puniorski Boulevards, has a circular hall with 5,000 seats and a revolving stage. Other conference halls also have simultaneous translation facilities.

Attached to the complex is a sports ground which stages a variety of international events.

◆◆
SEASIDE PARK
Beaches with warm mineral water shower facilities fringe this extensive park, with its Black Sea and Mediterranean varieties of flora and shrubs, its fountains, its Dolphinarium (in the northern part), Zoo, and (next to its central entrance) Copernicus Astronomy Complex. The Aquarium (at the

The casino at the Grand Hotel Varna, Sveti Konstantin, which also offers a range of spa treatments

park end of Seaside Park) contains native and exotic marine and freshwater species.

◆◆
MUSEUM OF ART AND HISTORY
Forty exhibition halls, including three showing artefacts from the celebrated Varna Necropolis. In 1972 more than a thousand gold objects dating from about 4,000BC were found in one of the Necropolis tombs, among them finely worked bracelets and necklets around the skeletal bones of a tribal chieftain. (Some of these unique items are periodically on tour to other museums.) Inhabited from the Stone Age, Varna area became the Greek colony of Odessos in the 6th century BC and was named Varna by the Slavs 12 centuries later. Traces of early Christian churches remain in Khan Krum Street and elsewhere. Ottoman dominance

Golden Sands, a major resort whose long, wide beaches are backed by hills and forests

was challenged by Crusaders under a Polish prince in 1444, and the first Russian assault, of 1828, resulted in two years of liberation. One of the first socialist groups was set up locally in the late 19th century.

ROMAN THERMAE
One of the biggest Roman ruins in Bulgaria, the 2nd-century baths, off K Bons I Boulevard, comprise cold, warm and hot chambers. An English-language guide book is on sale.

◆◆
STONE FOREST
An early natural formation, 50 million years old, apparently of stalagmite-type. Around 12 miles (20km) west on the road to Devnya.

Eating Out
Baikal, 9 Slivnitsa Street.
Galateya, Cape Galata.
Dimyat, 111 Primorski Boulevard.
Euxinograd, 2 Anton Ivanov Street.
Zlatnoto Pile, 7 Slivnitsa Boulevard.
Kotva, 29 Sari Stefano Street.
Komitovo Hanche, in the city's western part, at the start of the Hemus motorway.
Morsko Casino, near the Central Beach entrance.
Morsko Konche, Nezansimost Square.
Morska Sirena, at the Passenger Docks.
Morska Zvezda, on the terrace of the Central Sea Baths.
Nectar, 62 Primorski Boulevard.
Ocean, San Stefano Street.
Ostrava, 54 Dubrovnik Street.
Preslav, 1 Avram Gachev Street.
Pliska, on Red Square.

Pochivka, Primorski Boulevard, Pochivka bus stop.
Rostock, 20 Varnenchik Boulevard.
Sevastopol, on the corner of Slivnitsa and Primorski Boulevards.
Starata Kushta, 14 Druzki Street.
Horizont, in the Seaside Park, Akatsiite bus stop.
Chinarite, Ninth September Square.

Accommodation
Hotel Cherno More, 3-star, 35 Slivnitsa Boulevard (tel: 052 234088), part of the Interhotels chain. Three restaurants, one panoramic, on the 22nd floor. Ground floor café with terrace, day bar, congress halls, shops and a night club.
Hotel Odessa, 2-star, 1 Slivnitsa Boulevard (tel: 052 225312), right next to the Central Beach. Ground floor restaurant with terrace and café.
Hotel Musala, 1-star, 3 Musala Street (tel: 052 223925).
Orbita Youth Tourist Complex, off K Boris I Boulevard (tel: 052 225162).
Private lodgings and villas
Besides hotels, Balkantourist also offers accommodation at reasonably priced private lodgings and villas in the city suburbs and coastal villa zone.

Tourist Services Offices
Tourist services provided include: information, currency exchange, hotel reservations and accommodation in private lodgings, excursions inland and abroad, visits to folkstyle restaurants, night clubs, etc. Offices working all year round:
No 1, 3 Muaala Street.
No 2, 10 Avram Gachev Street.

No 3, 5 Tolbukhin Street.
No 4, 73 Primorski Boulevard.
No 5, Chaika Suburb, block 68 (Stadiona bus stop).
At Odessa Hotel - 1 Slivnitsa Boulevard.

KAMCHIYA
About 18 miles (30km) south of Varna, seaward of E87, is the mouth of the Kamchiya river, which flows through the Longoza nature reserve of forest and marsh which is rich in waterfowl.

Accommodation
The area has two hotels and a campsite.

Eating Out
There are four restaurants (including the **Nestinarka**, with barefoot fire-walking performances).

SUNNY BEACH
(Slunchev Bryag)
Bulgaria's big coastal holiday resorts are purpose-built rather than extensions (or ruinations) of existing native towns. They have been described as constituting 'the California of Eastern Europe'. What Bulgaria has, in fact, very sensibly done is capitalise on its sunny climate and its abundance of real estate. But it has not had to maximise site values with saturation development along the 4 miles (6km) of wide, fine-sand beach at Sunny Beach, for instance. And there is plenty of space and uncut tree foliage between its hotels, high-rise as many are.
Holiday prices are moderate, with packages including half-board and return flights. Local

'extras' are also low-cost. Sunny Beach (Slunchev Bryag anglicised) does not radically differ in park-like appearance from Golden Sands (Zlatni Pyasutsi) – except that the latter has 45 fewer hotels, and its wooded hills more closely approach the beach.

'Where Families Come First' is the motto of Sunny Beach, with its 122 hotels on a wide bay 20 miles (33km) north of Burgas. With summer water temperatures up to 75°F (24°C), the sea is shallow enough for bathing by small children, and there are lifeguard look-outs. Traffic is minimal along resort roads, and speed-limited, like the kiddie-trains. Playgrounds and kindergartens proliferate, staffed by trained personnel who speak foreign languages. Children's menus are featured in cafés and restaurants. Balkan Holidays' 'Kiddie Clubs' at the Club-Hotel Saturn and the Hotel Continental have nannies who organise fun activities and a baby patrol that checks children's rooms from 19.00 to midnight each weekday (see **Children**, pages 107-109 for full lists of relevant resort attractions.) Sporting amenities include sailing, boating, waterskiing, windsurfing, parascending, tennis, mini-golf, cycling, horse riding, and ten-pin bowling.

The Hotels Globus and Burgas

Meals are often accompanied by captivating displays of traditional singing and dancing

GOLDEN SANDS
BULGARIA

WHERE?

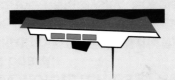

WHAT?

WHEN?

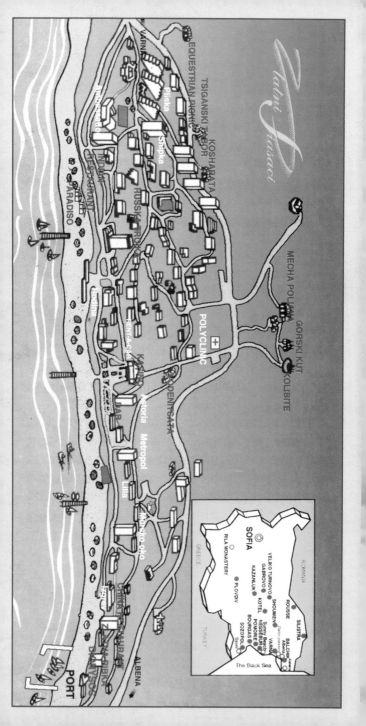

have mineral water treatment wards and swimming pools in operation year round.
(It is not usual for a holiday hotel to have its own pool, but there are several public ones.)

Sunny Beach Entertainment
Numerous hotels have discos or versatile bands who can turn out anything from folk, through golden oldies, to rock, soul and near-rap. There is disco dancing at the Rusalka, Zlatna Yabulka, Lazur and Melodia. Individual nightlife spots often offer varying degrees of folksiness or Bulgarian tradition. One can hardly imagine the average early Bulgar Khan being regaled with cocktails, psychedelic lights, rock music through echo-mikes and leggy showgirls in skimpy sequins as in the 'Khan's Tent' (Khanska Shatra). And the 'wine butt' at the Buchvata is fantasy sized. But there is a homelier atmosphere in the Chuchura (Fountain), which welcomes you with pre-menu bread-cakes and herb salt, plus music with intricate Balkan rhythms – and at the nearby Windmill (Vyaturna Melnitsa).
The floor show at the Yuzhni Noshti (Southern Nights) features exotic gypsy/oriental music and dances.
Biennially, in June, the Golden Orpheus international pop song festival is staged in Sunny Beach. This may include soulful ballads in a sort of Slavonic *Tom Jones* genre, but more contemporary western influences increasingly permeate.

Excursions
Through tour operators' representatives or hotel bureaux, hydrofoil trips and Balkantourist excursions can be booked to numerous destinations including Varna, Golden Sands, Veliko Turnovo and by ship, with a night on board, to Istanbul. There are buses to Nesebur, and taxis are inexpensive.

Accommodation
Reservations of hotel beds can be made through the Sunny Beach accommodation bureau in the town centre.
Zora Villas, fronting gentle tree-covered hills to the north of Sunny Beach, give something of the aspect of a garden suburb. There are three handy restaurants, a supermarket, bike-hire facilities and a regular mini-train service to the main parts of Sunny Beach. With basic cooking facilities, the villas are featured in tour operators' programmes – as is accommodation in the **Elenite Holiday Village**, a joint Bulgarian-Finnish development further north.

♦♦♦
NESEBUR (NESSEBUR) ✓

Nesebur is an ancient museum-town and fishing port which has somehow managed to retain its parochial appeal, despite the influx of sightseers from Sunny Beach, Bulgaria's biggest seaside resort 2 miles (3km) away. On a pretty promontory, it is reached by a narrow isthmus road, flanked by a windmill, and is easily

80

THE BLACK SEA

explored.
Weatherboarded houses
huddle around its cobbled
streets in almost as close
formation as the boats in its
small harbour. New ones have
been added in similar style,
with overhanging eaves and
small wooden balconies.
Traditionally furnished, these
provide accommodation,
available through tour
operators like Balkan Holidays,
for four to eight people who
breakfast in them but otherwise
eat out.
Nesebur was a very old-
established settlement when the
Greeks built up a colony here
called Mesembria in the 6th
century BC. The oldest of its
surprisingly numerous
churches (some ruined) are
from the 5th and 6th centuries
AD, and there are notable
Byzantine examples. The well
preserved 10th-century Church
of St John the Baptist, opposite
the 14th-century Church of the
Pantokrator, has 16th-and 17th-
century frescoes – as has the
10th-century St Stefan Church,
with its decorated bishop's
throne and pulpit. There is an
Archaeological Museum at the
west gate.

Eating Out
Street aromas of fried peppers
or *gyuvetch* vegetable hotpot
can be appetising. A
particularly atmospheric
restaurant is the **Captain's
Cabin (Kapitariska Shreshta)**,
as genuinely old as its
floorboards suggest, and one of
the comparatively few
establishments on the coast
specialising in seafood.

Accommodation
The Hotel Messambria, 2-star
(tel: 0554 3255), in the tiny
town's 'centre', is built in a
basically local style – only to
two storeys – and has a
restaurant, bar, and car rental
service. This hotel is often fully
booked, so it is worthwhile
telephoning ahead to see if they
have vacancies.

Balkantourist Office near the
port.

POMORIE
This is an ancient town which
produces a brandy and Dimyat
red dessert wine, salt from
extensive local pans, and
curative mud from a lagoon

Sunny Beach, the country's largest seaside resort, its many hotels dotted along the miles of beach

which sanatoria slap on to many an arthritis sufferer.

It has ancient foundations on a rocky peninsula. But a fire of 1906 destroyed much of its character, apart from a small area in the eastern part near the breakwater.

◆
AN EARLY TOMB
A mound near the town (opposite the Europa campsite). Something between a Thracian burial 'beehive' and a Roman mausoleum. Open to visitors except on Sunday.

Accommodation
The seaside **Hotel Pomorie**, 3-star (tel: 0596 2440), has a restaurant, pastry shop, and balneological section for the mud cure and other therapies. The **Europa campsite** is on the road towards Burgas, which is 13 miles (22km) west along E87.

Balkantourist Office
49 N Luskov Street.

BURGAS (BOURGAS)
Burgas is a largely industrial port, with a harbour for the country's oceanic fishing fleet, a petrochemical combine, and an international airport. It may be a staging post on some coach tours.

Its local sobriquet as 'the Chicago of Bulgaria' may be somewhat tongue-in-cheek. It has some spacious boulevards, a symphony orchestra, theatres, some low-rise apartment blocks, and traditional links with a stockbreeding and corn belt inland. But it does not look or feel like the inspiration for a Frank Sinatra song.

Accommodation
Hotel Bulgaria, 3-star, 21 Purvi Mai Street (tel: 056 45336), with panoramic restaurant, coffee shops, bars, nightclub, disco, and conference room with four-language simultaneous translation facilities.
Hotel Briz, 3-star (tel: 056 43191), near the railway station.
Hotel Primorets, 2-star (tel: 056 44117), near a beach.

Balkantourist Office
2 Alexandrosta Street (tel: 056 45553).
Union of Bulgarian Motorists
11 D Iliev Street.

82

THE BLACK SEA

SOZOPOL
Founded in 610BC as the Greek
settlement of Apollonia, Sozopol
is a picture-book museum town
and fishing port 21 miles (34km)
south of Burgas (which has an
international airport).
It is built on a rocky peninsula
fringed by small rocky islands,
but there are plenty of sandy
beaches in the vicinity, with
comfortable bathing in the sea
whose temperatures reach 75°F
(25°C) in July and August. There
is a laid-back, southern
atmosphere in its cobbled lanes
over which the wood-beamed
upper storeys of houses jut out
in neighbourly proximity. Near
the waterfront you can
sometimes buy local-style fish
(probably small mackerel) and
chips in paper wrapping to eat
as you walk around.
Extra tone and colour is lent in
the first half of September when
the Apollonia Arts Festival
stages music, drama, pictorial
art, cinematic and poetry
events, attracting poets, actors,
artists and architects both from
Bulgaria and abroad. The spirit
of Apollo, Greek god of music,
song and poetry, lives on.

ROPOTAMO RIVER
From Sozopol excursions may
be made to the River Ropotamo.
Reaching the sea just before
Cape Maslen Nos, about 11
miles (18km) south, the
Ropotamo has banks flanked
with deciduous trees often
linked together with creeping
vines. A row-boat trip along it
only gently disturbs its water-
lilies, large dragonflies, and

perhaps less familiar forms of
water life. Details are available
from the Balkantourist office.

Accommodation
The Balkantourist office may be
able to find 'village rooms' in
one of the old weatherboarded
houses. Otherwise, **Dyuni**
holiday village is a handy base.
Zlatna Ripka campsite is about
1.5 miles (2.5km) north of
Sozopol, on the way to
Chernomorets, by the coast.

Balkantourist Office
Chervenoarmeiska Street (tel:
378).

DYUNI
Dyuni (or Düni) is a new
purpose-built holiday village
about 3 miles (5km) south of
Sozopol, mainly on a hillside a
little way landward of coastal
sand dunes, a quiet setting for
families.

Eating Out
There are various individual
restaurants and bars for late-
night carousel. The **Moryashka
Kruchma** (Sailor's Inn) features
seafood, and the **Starata Loza**
(Old Vine) has a nightly folklore
show from 22.00.

Accommodation
There are five small low-rise 3-
star hotels, self-catering
accommodation in 'Fishermen's
Huts' and 'Sozopol Houses', the
Port Village on the beach itself,
and the newly opened Club
Village 'built in the style of the
Bulgarian monasteries'.
Holidays here can be arranged
by tour operators.
The nearby **campsite**, a 3-star
with 1,000 capacity, has a
restaurant, café, and shops.

THE DANUBE (DUNAV) AND THE NORTH

PLEVEN

Pleven marked a decisive turning-point in Bulgaria's liberation from Turkish Rule when, in 1877, 40,000 Russians and Romanians were among those who died in their capture of the city from Osman Pasha.

◆◆
PANORAMA OF THE EPIC OF PLEVEN

This painting, on a vast canvas, stretches right round the inside of the dome of a tall 1977 building on a hilltop of Skobelev Park. A wide 'shelf' around a high viewing platform gives the impression of extending the painting into the foreground, with recreated trenches, cannon, and burnt-out ammunition carts which (electrically) give a realistic effect of glowing embers. The panorama, illustrating with thousands of figures the various assaults all around the city in

Pleven, a bustling administrative and industrial centre with a rich historical past dating back to the 4th century BC

1877, is about as large as that in Volgograd, USSR, devoted to the World War II siege of Stalingrad. Pleven's was designed by Soviet and Bulgarian artists, who had local volunteer help.

Excursions

A bus from the centre of town takes visitors to **Kailuka Park**. As well as a leisure complex, this contains a memorial monument to Jews who died in 1944 in a fire at their internment camp here.
Connected by rail with Sofia, Ruse (Rousse) and Varna, Pleven is an industrial and administrative centre, and sightseeing interest is mainly in monuments and museums.

Accommodation

Hotel Pleven, 3-star, 2 Republika Square (tel: 064

THE DANUBE AND THE NORTH

20062), with restaurant, bar, night club, information bureau and car rental office.

Balkantourist Office 3 San Stefano Street (tel: 064 24119). Car repairs 2 Industrialna Street.
Union of Bulgarian Motorists 6a Radetski Street.

◆
NIKOPOL
Today an agricultural/industrial town and Danube hydrofoil stop, Nikopol had a Roman fortress in 169AD and Byzantine successor from 629.
The fortifications of Bash-Tabia Kale that remain, in ruins, are those erected by King Ivan, who made Nikopol his unofficial capital during the medieval Second Bulgarian Kingdom.

◆
SVISHTOV
With a harbour on a bend of the Danube, Svishtov is the birthplace of Aleko Konstantinov, who wrote of folk-life in the 19th century when Svishtov was a pre-eminent commercial centre. He was also dubbed 'founder of the Bulgarian tourist movement'. Local sightseeing includes **Aleko Konstaninov Museum**, 17th-century churches of St Dimiter and SS Peter and Paul, 19th-century churches by the self-taught master-builder Kolyo Ficheto, and the town's clocktower.

Accommodation
Hotel Dunav, 1-star, with Balkantourist office.
Hotel Aleko, 1-star, with Bulgarian-style tavern.

◆◆
RUSE (ROUSSE)
Bulgaria's fourth city, and a major port visited by Danube cruisers, Ruse is rather handsomely set on terraces above the river. The Bridge of Friendship to the northeast is an entry point to Bulgaria with offices handling passports, customs, currency exchange, petrol coupons and tourist information. The bridge is also known as the Danube Bridge. On the other side is Romania which, together with Bulgaria, constructed the bridge in 1954. The Romans built a 1st-century fortress here at Sexaginta Pristia (port of 60 vessels), which had been a fishing village for about 5,000 years. Barbarians sacked around the 6th century and new medieval fortress was destroyed by 14th-century Turks, who built their citadel of Roustchouk. The Romanians helped the Russians in their final assaults of 1878 against the Turks in these parts.
Ruse is important industrially, with its shipyard and major manufacture of farm machinery – and culturally, with its international March Musical Weeks, opera, art gallery, and national museum of transport. (Bulgaria's first railway linked Ruse and Varna.)
There are echoes of Vienna, Budapest and Bucharest in its older streets' Baroque, Renaissance, and *fin-de-siècle* architecture. The parks and sports stadia (three) are vast, as are some modern memorial monuments.
Whiffs of chlorine gas and other

wind-blown fumes that the visitor to Ruse might notice are likely to be from the vast chemical plant on the Romanian bank at Giurgiu, said to be one of the major polluters of the Danube.

Eating Out

The Leventa restaurant near the TV Tower, is in a former Turkish arsenal and features the national style of a different Danubian country in each of its seven rooms.

The Lipnik park outside Ruse has a rowing lake, and the folk-style **Ovtcharska Luka** restaurant which serves lamb specialities.

Excursions

ROCK CHURCHES AND MONASTIC CELLS

Near the village of Ivanovo, 14 miles (23km) south of Ruse, and in the scenic canyon of the Rusenski Lom river. These ruins contain biographical murals from the 12th to14th centuries, which include a portrait of the Bulgarian King Ivan Alexander. Best preserved is the Archangel Church.

Accommodation

Hotel Riga, 3-star (tel: 082 22181), with restaurant, bar and pastry shop.
Hotel Dunav, 2-star (tel: 082 26518), with restaurant, bar, tavern in national style and pastry shop.
Hotel Bulgaria, 1-star, bookings through Balkantourist office (see below).

Balkantourist Office 1 Raiko Daskalov Street (tel: 082 33629).

Union of Bulgarian Motorists
45 General Skobelev Street.

SILISTRA

Danube industrial port and hydrofoil stop, Silistra was founded in the 2nd century AD by the Roman Emperor Trajan. A **Roman tomb**, with a wealth of very well preserved wall-paintings from the 4th century, is the most interesting of the town's surviving historical sites, which include Roman and Turkish fortifications.

The **District Historical Museum** is in an old local house. One of Silistra's factories produces souvenirs.

Excursions

Important sightseeing attractions in the region are Lake Sreburna nature reserve and the Thracian tomb near Sveshtari (see below).

Accommodation

Hotel Zlatna Dobruja, 2-star, Georgi Dimitrov Street, with restaurant, in main street. Book through Balkantourist.

Balkantourist Office

7 Svoboda Square Church (tel: 082 23990).
Union of Bulgarian Motorists
12 Docho Mikhaylov Street.

TUTRAKAN

A port and fishing centre about halfway between Ruse and Silistra, and once a Roman fortress, Tutrakan has a unique museum devoted to Danubian fishing and boat-building.

LAKE SREBURNA

This nature reserve, about 12 miles (20km) west of Silistra, is included on a UNESCO world list of valued natural sites. 'The Eldorado of the Wading Birds' is what the 19th-century Hungarian traveller Felix Kanitz called it. The lake's reed-and-rush-covered islands are nesting grounds for 90 varieties of birds, and are visited by almost as many migrants – including pelicans, in autumn. Sightseers' group visits can be arranged through Balkantourist.

◆◆
SVESHTARI THRACIAN TOMB

Discovered in 1982, this tomb near Isperih and Koubrat on the Silistra-Rargrad road has been described by a Bulgarian archaeologist as 'not just a remarkable monument of Thracian art, but.... also.... one of the most outstanding works of Hellenistic art in general'. The architecture, funerary rites, murals and sculptures in the tomb, which has an entrance passage and three chambers under a mound, convince experts that it was that of a Thracian king and queen of the 3rd century BC – although it was looted in early times. Paintings depict a noble horseman and his armed attendants being approached by a goddess who hands him a gold wreath and is followed by four women carrying gifts such as a perfume box and a jewellery case.

Ten stone caryatids, decoratively dressed female figures supporting an architrave, are considered to be of exceptional interest. Each has an individually sculpted face, and they are expected eventually to reveal to researchers a great deal about the symbolism of female figures in Thracian religion and arts. With no local tourist accommodation, Sveshtari might be visited from Ruse or Shumen. Further information is available from Balkantourist.

The Thracians were keen horsemen, as depicted in their art. Below: 4th-3rd century BC tomb mural at Kazanluk

PEACE AND QUIET

Wildlife and Countryside in Bulgaria
by Paul Sterry

Bulgaria is a country of contrasting landscapes. There are vast tracts of wild and inaccessible mountains which remain largely unspoiled, but in the lowlands most of the fertile land of the plains is devoted to farming. Vineyards, olive groves and orchards of fruit trees are vital elements of the Bulgarian landscape.

The Black Sea coast is a major tourist region, and in some areas this has had a devastating effect on the wildlife. Freshwater lakes at Varna and Burgas have been modified by hydro-electric schemes and by saltpans to such an extent that most of the breeding birds have disappeared. However, they still present probably the best

Secretive and untamable creatures, wildcats make their lairs between boulders and among tree-roots

chances in Europe of seeing white and Dalmatian pelicans, which stop off on migration. Mountain ranges dominate the south and the west of the country, with many peaks remaining snow-capped throughout the year. Their lower slopes are heavily wooded and have a wide variety of woodland birds and scarce and endangered mammals such as the European brown bear and wolf.

The Northern Black Sea Coast

The Black Sea coast is a popular tourist destination which has been developed considerably over the last 25 years. Nevertheless, there are still areas rich in wildlife which are often noticeably different from those further south where the influence of the Mediterranean is still felt. Here, the plants, and to some extent the animals, too, are central European in origin. Either side of the town of Balchik, the coast road passes by chalk cliffs and rolling

hillsides. The grassy slopes are covered in flowers such as milk vetches, sages, brooms, pinks and the paeony *Paeonia peregrina* and the cliffs to the south of the town have good populations of alpine swift and black-headed bunting. They are also a well-known haunt of the pied wheatear, an elegant, black and white summer visitor with a mainly Asiatic distribution – this is its only regular breeding site in Europe. Further up the coast to the north, the road passes more cliffs where rollers, rock thrushes and eagle owls breed, and eventually leads to Cape Kaliakra, 15 miles (25km) north of Balchik. The grassy fields slope towards the sea, ending in sheer cliffs, 230 feet (70m) high. Although a popular tourist spot and 'managed' as such, a rich variety of interesting plants, such as showy paeonies, stocks, sages and irises can be found. Cape Kaliakra is an excellent migration spot with unusual Asiatic birds turning up from March to May and in August and September. It is a good point from which to watch seabird movements in the Black Sea, and shearwaters, gulls and terns can be numerous. Because of the crumbly nature of the soil, the cliffs are riddled with caves both above and below the surface of the water. Egyptian vultures, rose-coloured starlings and eagle owls use them as nesting sites on land, whereas at sea level they provide shelter for one of the last remaining colonies of the endangered monk seal. To the south of Balchik, at the

mouth of the River Batova, lies the Forest of Baltata. Although its wildlife interest has been severely reduced by man, it still has collared flycatchers, sombre tits, hawfinches and many other woodland birds, as well as small numbers of wild boar.

The Southern Black Sea Coast
The inviting waters of the Black Sea and the almost Mediterranean climate have made the southeastern coast of Bulgaria popular with residents and tourists alike. While this has had serious impact on the wildlife and the coast itself, the land a few miles away from the resorts is relatively unspoiled. Inland from the coastal town of Burgas are three lakes, Mandra, Burgas and Atanasov, now drastically altered by recent developments. Lake Atanasov is used in the extraction and purification of salt and the saline conditions are greatly to the liking of birds such as avocets and black-winged stilts. Of the other two, Lake Burgas still attracts many migrants during spring and autumn but its reedbeds no longer harbour many breeding birds. White and Dalmatian pelicans, glossy ibises and spoonbills all pass through regularly and little egrets and white storks are a familiar feature of the shallow margins of the Lake Burgas. Particularly in spring, Mediterranean and little gulls are numerous, looking smart with their near black hoods and white eye rings. Mediterranean gulls are especially attractive with their pure white wings and

Despite their immense size, eagle owls are difficult to see since they nest in remote forests and on high cliffs

are easily distinguished by their loud 'cow-cow' calls. At the right time of year, marsh terns and waders can be abundant. The Istranca Mountains run from the Bosphorous in Turkey into southeast Bulgaria and have woodlands which are easily reached from the coast. A mixture of oak, beech, elm, sycamore and lime create interesting forests which still harbour wolves, wildcats and pine and beech martens. The latter two species are extremely agile predators which are equally at home in the trees and on the ground. Although shy, they are sometimes seen in car headlights when crossing the road. In clearings, medlars and tree heathers tower over hellebores, sages, crocuses, tulips and other colourful flowers.

During spring and autumn migration large numbers of seabirds pass the Bulgarian coastline on their travels through the Black Sea. Shearwaters, gulls and terns are most easily seen is an onshore breeze is blowing, while cormorants and shags are always in evidence. During the winter months the Bulgarian shores harbour black-throated divers and great-crested grebes.

Lakes and Marshes
Before the growth of the

PEACE AND QUIET

population along the coast and the development of the tourist industry, there were interesting lakes along the length of the Black Sea. Nowadays, however, man has influenced many of them to such an extent that they have lost much of their wildlife interest.

The lakes at Burgas and Lake Varna near Balchik no longer have the vast numbers of breeding birds they once did. However, during migration times they swarm with birds. Swallows and martins stop off to feed on insects, and flocks of cranes call in briefly, particularly in March. During May, hundreds of marsh terns pass through, most in full breeding plumage. Whiskered terns and distinctive black terns are a wonderful sights as they hawk for insects, but most elegant of all is the white-winged black tern, with its pure white tail and black and white wings.

The course of the mighty River Danube, flanked by riverine forest, marks the northern border of Bulgaria with Romania. The river is most famous for its delta, but the floodplain along its course is also of major importance. Near the town of Silistra in northeast Bulgaria there are several large, reed-fringed lakes which support vast colonies of breeding birds.

One of these, Lake Sreburna (see page 85), 12 miles (20km) west of Silistra is now a nature reserve, mainly on account of its breeding population of Dalmatian pelicans. Despite limited access to the reserve itself, most of the wildlife can easily be seen from the surrounding countryside. Throughout its reedbeds, colonies of little egret, little bittern, purple, night grey and squacco herons breed in

Small flocks of white pelicans often grace the shores of Bulgaria's lakes on migration in spring and autumn

profusion and marsh harriers quarter the land in search of prey. Twenty-eight species of mammal have been recorded on the reserve including hamster, souslik, and the bizarre subterranean mole rat. The marshes surrounding these lakes and along the length of the Danube have different birds. Meadows are still the haunt of the corncrake, a declining bird throughout Europe, and black-headed wagtails nest in grassy tussocks. Surely the smartest of all the races of yellow wagtail, the male is resplendent with yellow plumage and black hood.

Ropotamo National Park

Lying 31 miles (50km) south of Burgas on the Black Sea coast of Bulgaria, the Ropotamo National Park protects an extensive area of riverine forest around the mouth of the River Ropotamo. Lakes and sand dunes add to its interest and although popular with tourists and fishermen alike, there is still much of interest to the wildlife enthusiast. The riverine forest is of a type now rare in Bulgaria and contains a mosaic of deciduous trees such as oak, ash, poplar, elm and alder, most with their 'feet' in water. Climbers like ivy and clematis reach skyward and clearings become a riot of tangled undergrowth with butterflies flitting through the dappled sunlight. In swampy areas, penduline tits weave their curious, bottle-shaped nests, suspended from branches, while in areas of dense foliage red-breasted and collared flycatchers and golden orioles

provide tantalisingly brief views in the canopy. Birds of prey are often seen circling above the tree tops and nest in the cover of the leaf canopy. Hobbies and black kites both occur in small numbers and even the occasional pair of saker or white-tailed eagle can be found. The latter is unmistakable, with a wingspan of nearly 8 feet (240cm), a conspicuous white tail in the adults and a silhouette in flight which resembles a barn-door.

The lake region of Arkutino, is a good place for water birds and water insects, most notably mosquitoes! The introduced, pink-flowered *Nelumbo nucifera* with its lily-like leaves provide shade for the fish, frogs and other aquatic life below. Purple and night herons are common, the latter preferring to roost during the day and feed at dawn and dusk.

Around the mouth of the river a system of sand dunes is threatened by increased camping pressure. However, the wet and dry dune slacks and stabilised dunes have a remarkable array of coastal plants, some of which are widespread in Europe, while others are distinctly local. Marram grass, sea beet, sea knotgrass, sea holly and cottonweed are all common and low bushes of thorn of Christ, *Paliurus spina-christi*, remind the careless stroller of their presence with their fierce spines.

Woodlands

Much of lowland Bulgaria has long-since been cleared of

PEACE AND QUIET

woodland and turned into agricultural land, leaving only the riverine forests at the mouths of a few rivers flowing into the Black Sea. However, the slopes of most of the mountain ranges are still wooded and Bulgaria takes a certain pride in its forests, many lying in national parks or forest reserves.

On the lower slopes of the hills and mountains, the woodland usually comprises deciduous trees such as beech, hazel, oak and lime, sometimes with a shrubby understorey of juniper and privet. Depending on the amount of human disturbance, they may hold interesting mammals such as red and roe deer, polecat, badger and pine and stone martens.

Woodland birds abound, with jay, turtle dove, short-toed treecreeper and golden oriole being common. Smaller numbers of sombre tits, olive-tree warblers and hawfinches also occur, but are difficult to see. High in the canopy the delightful little red-breasted flycatcher flits from leaf to leaf in search of caterpillars. Its sharp call often gives its presence away and when in view its robin-like breast is obvious as is its habit of flicking its tail. It shares this habitat with its relative, the collared flycatcher. Unfortunately for the birdwatcher, the race which occurs in Bulgaria lacks the complete white collar which distinguishes it from the pied flycatcher of northern Europe. However, the latter only occurs in Bulgaria on passage and so any black and white flycatcher seen is likely to be collared.

The heavy shade produced by many of the deciduous trees, and in particular by beach, discourages most understorey plants: there is not enough light for them to photosynthesise. Some flowers overcome this by growing before there are leaves on the trees, while others have become saprophytic, which means they feed on decaying, underground leaf litter, using a fungal partner. The ghost orchid takes this to an extreme, spending almost all its life underground and flowering for no more than a few days. Even then a plant may not flower every year and only does so when conditions are exactly right.

The Rhodope Mountains

The Rhodope Mountain chain lies along the northern side of the Bulgarian border with Greece between two rivers, the Maritsa and the Mesta. Although the landscape comprises gently rounded hills and valleys, the peak of Great Perelik rises to nearly 7,200 feet (2,200m) and over 5,000 acres (2,000ha) of land are protected by national park status.

The lower slopes are cloaked in deciduous woodland consisting of beech, hornbeam and oak which are the haunt of many woodland birds. Chaffinches search for insects and fallen seeds, but the hawfinch, with its massive beak. is the only woodland resident able to crack the hard seeds of the hornbeam. In the spring, golden orioles, redstarts and nightingales – all loud songsters – contribute to the woodland chorus of bird song.

Higher up the slopes, the deciduous trees are replaced by pines and spruce, under whose dense canopy one-leaved wintergreen, two-leaved squill, herb paris and coralroot bittercress often flourish. Firecrests sing their high-pitched songs from the tree canopy and crossbills noisily feed on ripe pine cones. These higher woodlands harbour secretive mammals such as brown bear, wolf and wild boar. They manage to survive in these hills, not so much because they are protected from hunting, but because the terrain is so inaccessible. Consider yourself extremely fortunate if you see even one of these animals. Rocky outcrops among the higher regions of forest are dotted with cranesbills, saxifrages and vetches and are the haunt of the elegant rock bunting. The male birds with their chestnut bodies and grey, white and black-striped heads sing a delightful buzzing song from rocks and branches, and sometimes in flight.

Some areas of forest have been cleared for timber and the resulting clearings, as well as the natural glades, are good for wild flowers and butterflies. Meadow rues, St John's worts, sages and foxgloves are a delight after the shade of the woodland.

In the deep shade of Bulgaria's forest the extraordinary ghost orchid appears in the summer months

PEACE AND QUIET

The Cherni Vrukh Mountains

The mountains of the Cherni Vrukh National Park lie only a short distance south of Sofia and are both attractive and good for wildlife, with over 100 species of bird having been recorded. Within the 57,000 acres (23,000ha) of the park, two reserves at Bistrishko Branishte and Torfeno Branishte protect areas of spruce woodland and marshy moorland respectively. Because of its close proximity to Sofia and heavy snowfall in winter, Cherni Vrukh is a popular ski resort with its centre at Aleko. Despite the disturbance, alpine choughs and alpine accentors often feed close to the buildings, seemingly indifferent to people. Other outdoor pursuits are catered for here, and there are several route-marked trails for trekkers. The park has the advantage of allowing easy access to all the zones of vegetation found in Bulgarian mountains, from deciduous forest at low altitudes to alpine meadows and the snow line. Beautiful clear lakes and rivers and dwarf mountain pine forest add to its wildlife interest. The higher slopes of the hills are covered in pines and spruce which create the dense shade much favoured by deer and wild boar. The woods also host an even more secretive animal which is occasionally surprised near its lair or at a kill. The wildcat certainly lives up to its name and has a reputation of being completely untamable. The lair is usually among an outcrop of boulders or under fallen trees and here the

Eagle Owls

On remote and inaccessible rocky outcrops and deep gorges in Cherni Vrukh, eagle owls still nest and rear their young. Despite their immense size, they are very difficult to spot because they remain motionless during the day and their plumage helps them blend in with the surroundings. Often the first sign of the presence of an eagle owl is its deep, far-carrying 'boo-hoo' call uttered at dusk. If you are lucky, you may see the bird take to the wing as the light fades, off in search of its prey, which includes animals the size of roe deer! They tend to return to roost in the same spot each morning, even when not nesting, which gives the persistent observer opportunities for a prolonged view.

females rear their kittens in the early summer.

The Rila Mountains

Lying 60 miles (100km) south of Sofia in southwest Bulgaria, the Rila Mountains contain rugged and beautiful landscapes with many towering peaks above 8,000 feet (2,500m), the highest of which, at nearly 10,000 feet (3,000m), is Musala. Within the boundaries of the national park, more than 150 lakes, heavily wooded hillsides and alpine meadows also add to the scenic appeal of the area.

The well known monastery at Rila (see page 39) is a good starting point from which to explore the area. Rushing rivers carve deep gorges in the

The elegant, trumpet-shaped flowers of Gentiana pyrenaica *are found at high altitudes in the Rila Mountains*

hillsides and grey wagtails and dippers are ever present. The latter characteristically bob up and down on rocks in the water and submerge in search of food. Hornbeam, beech, oak and mountain ash cloak the lower slopes of the mountains and merge with Scots and Macedonian pines and spruces at higher altitudes. Among the branches and leaves, birds such as crested tit, firecrest, nutcracker and crossbill forage for food, while on the woodland floor, rare and secretive capercaillie and hazelhen keep to the darkest shade in the company of red and roe deer. In glades and clearings, flowers such as leopardsbane, cranesbills, lungworts and saxifrages appear during the summer months, while at higher altitudes grass of Parnassus, sticky catchfly, marsh marigold and bistort are found in damp hollows.

At around 6,500 feet (2,000m), just below the snow line, alpine meadows are a riot of colour from June to August with the beautiful gentian *Gentiana pyrenaica*, buttercups, milk vetches, Snowdon lily, moss campion and several speedwells. Birds that might be seen include alpine accentors, searching for insects and seeds in bare, open patches. These are sometimes accompanied by rock buntings and shore larks, the latter with their yellow throats and black, feathery 'horns'.

The slopes below support open woodlands of dwarf mountain pine and underneath the light canopy crocuses, gentians, purple coltsfoot and mountain avens grow in the rocky soil.

Vikhren Park

The Vikhren National Park lies 30 miles (50km) south of Rila in southwest Bulgaria. It contains

PEACE AND QUIET

over 16,500 acres (6,700ha) of mountainous country in the Pirin range which itself runs down to the Greek border. Although the park holds extensive areas of woodland cloaking the lower slopes, over half its area can be considered as 'alpine' in nature. Not surprisingly, it includes some of the highest peaks in the whole of the Pirin Mountain range, the highest being Mount Vikhren at nearly 10,000 feet (3,000m).

The lower slopes are covered in a mixture of beech, spruce and Balkan pine and much of the woodland is completely unspoiled. The oldest tree in the park is thought to be a Balkan pine which grows at the foot of Mount Vikhren at an altitude of 6,500 feet (2,000m) and is estimated to be 1,280 years old. These mixed woodlands are the haunt of many species of bird as well as forest mammals such as red and roe deer, brown bear, wolf and wildcat. Above the highest tracts of dwarf mountain pine are

Capercaillie
The capercaillie is the largest woodland bird found in Vikhren Park. Despite the fact that the males are over 30 inches (80cm) long, they are extremely wary and difficult to see and the utmost stealth is required. The best time to search for them is in early summer when the males advertise themselves with an extraordinary display. The tail is raised and fanned out, and the bird utters some amazing sounds: first a loud rattle, followed by what sounds like a cork being pulled from a bottle, and lastly a loud crashing noise.

extensive alpine meadows. Many of the flowers are endemic to the Bulgarian mountains, while others are widespread in the Alps, the

Beautifully marked Balkan wall lizards are found in woodland clearings and in open country where they feed on insects

Large colonies of wood ants are a conspicuous feature of Bulgaria's forests and are considered beneficial insects

Pyrenees and even northern Europe. Alpine bistort, saxifrages, milk vetches, alpine bartsia, pyramidal bugle, purple coltsfoot and bellflowers put on a colourful display. Some areas boast rocky, limestone outcrops which harbour a different variety of flowers, including violets, saxifrages, mountain avens and gentians.

Open Country, Forests and Agricultural Land

Much of lowland Bulgaria is devoted to agriculture and the country is justly famous for its bottled fruits and jams. Elsewhere, land has been given over to grazing by goats. While most of the plants and animals that were originally found there have declined, others have benefited from the changes. Rollers, bee-eaters and lesser grey shrikes perch on overhead wires and find open agricultural land a rich and easy feeding area. Balkan wall lizards, grasshoppers and bush crickets scurry across the broken soil, frequently falling victim to these keen-eyed predators. Tawny pipits and crested, short-toed and calandra larks work the furrows in ploughed fields in search of uprooted grubs. Wherever there are orchards or trees and scrub, red-backed shrikes, olivaceous and barred warblers, scop's owls and cirl buntings nest in the cover and shade they provide. If the ground vegetation is lush and grassy, corncrakes and quail sing their respective songs, whereas barren areas are favoured by stone-curlews and little and great bustards. Although bustards still try to breed in Bulgaria in small numbers, during the winter there is usually an influx of

PEACE AND QUIET

White storks frequently build their untidy nests on roofs and poles

these birds from northeast Europe and Asia.

White storks have benefited from man's buildings and structures throughout Europe and nests on top of buildings, churches and telegraph poles are a familiar sight in Bulgaria. The birds return annually to these nests in March after spending the winter in Africa and feed in fields and marshes in the surrounding country. These nests are ramshackle affairs of twigs and domestic rubbish, often used by other birds at the same time. In some particularly large nests Spanish, tree and house sparrows can all breed side by side like tenants in the storks' cellars!

Along the coast herring gulls sometimes noisily nest on rooftops and are certainly not as welcome as would be a stork's nest. Syrian woodpeckers are regular, if rather surprising visitors to most of Bulgaria's towns. They can often be seen flying down the road from one telegraph pole to another in search of grubs.

Although most of Bulgaria's forests lie on inaccessible slopes high in the mountains, the lower slopes are often exploited for timber. However, the country treats its forests as a natural asset and felling is strictly controlled.

Wood Ants

The Bulgarians have a healthy respect for one of the forest's smallest but most important residents, the wood ant. This industrious insect forms large colonies in huge mounds of leaf litter and pine needles, and foraging parties spread out in every direction. Although less than half an inch (a centimetre or so) long, these creatures have a formidable bite and can spray formic acid at an intruder. There are not many animals that will take them on *en masse*. Foresters consider them to be invaluable in the woodlands because they are strictly carnivorous, collecting caterpillars, bugs, sawfly larvae and anything else they can tackle (all these creatures would damage the trees in one way or another). The prey is then carried back to the nest where it is dismembered and fed to the growing larvae safely housed inside the ant hill. Not surprisingly, wood ants are protected by the law.

SHOPPING

Ceramic pots on a market stall

Souvenirs of a Bulgarian holiday will probably consist, in the main, of folklore artefacts in which the country specialises; like its musical traditions, Bulgaria's craftwork is still very much alive. 'Touristic' souvenirs include glazed ceramic vases, plates and ashtrays with swirling patterns around mystical 'eyes' (most usually on a brown background, but sometimes in attractive greens and blues); wrought-iron and copper articles; carved and sculpted wooden caskets, bowls, plates and spoons; folk-music instruments, decorated wooden phials containing attar of roses, and dolls in various regional costumes.

The dolls are usually demure and chocolate-boxy, but children with a taste for the bizarre may appreciate the grotesquely masked models of Koukeri – folk-dancers whose role is to scare off evil spirits. Hand or machine-embroidered blouses, tablecloths and runners, homespun fabrics and knitwear are available and there are traditional-style rugs. Costume jewellery in silver and other metals can be inexpensive. Jackets and coats in fur, sheepskin, leather or suede can be good buys.

The occasional Corecom shop, in the bigger hotels or self-contained in the resorts, usually sell many or all of the items above – plus imported goods, including radios, cameras, perfumes, spirits, liqueurs and cigarettes. There are plenty of other shops, including music stores selling cheap records and cassettes.

Sofia is naturally one of the best cities for shopping, and facilities there are listed on pages 25-26. Be prepared: photographic film, especially for colour slides and cassette cameras, is hard to find outside Sofia and the bigger resorts on the Black Sea. The enthusiastic photographer should bring along a good supply of this.

FOOD AND DRINK

While many of the raw materials speak for themselves as to quality and exceptional budget value, food and drink in tourist Bulgaria are often presented in a sort of show-business production. Fire-walkers, gypsy dancers and singing shepherds are just a few of the speciality accompaniments to meals or liqueurs in folklore restaurants, which are done up with a variety of rustic or 'traditional' props and trappings. 'International' cuisine is provided in most resort hotels, with menus in several languages, though Bulgarian dishes are not likely to be too spicy or strongly flavoured for most palates – and are particularly inexpensive at a *mehana* (a tavern, which may not offer a wide choice). **Tea** is usually green, often Chinese, and served without milk. Expresso **coffee** is available from some hotel bars. Otherwise, coffee may be like Turkish, with thick grounds. Many visitors bring supplies of familiar tea-bags, instant coffee and powdered milk.

Bulgaria's climate, soils and varied terrain enable her to raise superb **vegetables**, salads, peaches, strawberries, cherries, apples – and

Bulgarian dishes (the Shopska salad is sprinkled with grated white sheep's cheese), accompanied by Bulgarian wine

Bulgarian Specialities

Shopska salad – 'Shopska' means Sofia-style, and it is usually chopped tomato, onion, cucumber and pickled pepper, seasoned with salt, sunflower oil and vinegar, and topped with flakes of ewesmilk cheese and parsley.

Kypolou – a puree of aubergines with peppers, tomatoes and garlic.

Tarator – cold soup of sliced cucumber, walnuts, garlic and dill in yoghurt (which is reckoned to prevent 'garlic breath').

Kebap – meat cut in small portions and simmered in a rich sauce (whereas *kebapcheta* are grilled mincemeat portions).

Gyuvech – usually a stew with vegetables, herbs and meats. (Gyuvech is also the name of the earthenware casserole.)

Drob Sarma – a lamb pilaff prepared with eggs, onions and yoghurt.

Sarmi – vine or cabbage leaves stuffed with minced veal, pork, onions, paprika, herbs and rice.

Banitsa – hot cheese pastry (sometimes with spinach).

Mekitsas – batter fried in oil; can be flavoured with cheese, jam or honey and walnuts.

---

abundant grapes of several types.

The country produces about 500 million litres of **wine** a year, of a quality which attracts exports to 70 countries and fulsome testimonials from leading Western experts.

Among **meats**, lamb is usually the most succulent. But beef and veal may sometimes seem

FOOD AND DRINK

ESTATE BOTTLED ℮ 75cl

Bulgarian

Chardonnay

PRESLAV REGION

A fine white wine

11.5% vol

Produced and bottled in Bulgaria by Vinimpex. Sofia

Sole importer in the UK BULGARIAN VINTNERS Co. Ltd. London N1 9RD.

The country's wines are increasingly exported and enjoyed. In Bulgaria itself the labels may well be in Cyrillic script

tough by western standards – though it is another matter with any meat slowly cooked in an earthenware casserole.

Chicken is often free range. Pork is tasty served in stews, *kebapcheta* (oblong rissoles) or *kyufteta* (meatballs).

Black Sea **fish** are not notable – except as prepared in a few speciality restaurants along the coast. A type of mackerel and grey mullet are what normally seem available. Trout from mountain streams or lakes are good. Carp and pike-perch are available in some areas, while cod and other sea fish are brought in by Bulgaria's oceanic fleet.

Wines

Bottled wines sold in Bulgarian restaurants are often labelled with fanciful local names which, furthermore, are in Cyrillic script. But (in seaside resorts and big cities especially) waiters can usually advise as to their grape types.

These can be the wines now enjoying popularity in the west: the full-bodied red *Cabernet* (winner of nearly 150 gold medals in international competitions), the lighter, smooth *Merlot*, the outstanding dry white *Chardonnay* (especially Khan Krum), and various Rieslings.

But there are also distinctly Bulgarian varieties, notably: *Mavrud*, deep and fruity, ageing well; *Gamza*, with a slightly resinous flavour when young. a fine bouquet with age; *Pamid*, a light red rather like a young Rhone wine; *Melnik*, dark red and velvety, and the *Misket* medium white from Karlovo or Sungulare.

Dessert wines include *Slavianka* and *Vratsa Misket*.

'Champanska' sparklers are *Iskra*, and the pink *Magura*. Reasonable brandies are *Pliska*, *Preslav* and *Pomorie*. The plumbrandy, *slivova*, can in quantity produce a thundering hangover for which a local prescription is yoghurt (*kisselo mlyako*) night and morning. This may also be needed after indulgence in anise-flavoured *masticka* and *raki*.

Bulgarian bottled beers are cheap, and taste so, though some *mehani* and seafront bars sell quite a wholesome lager type on draught. Pricey German and Dutch beers, Scotch and London gin are available in the bars of many of the larger hotels.

Bottled fruit juices are plentiful and inexpensive.

The Bulgarian for 'Cheers' is *Naz drave* (drah-vay).

ACCOMMODATION

Bulgaria progressively updates its hotels, restaurants and other facilities. However, within nationally graded categories, hotel standards are not yet as uniform and predictable as those of major international hotel chains.

In other countries, self-catering accommodation is often in atmospheric touring areas inland. In contrast to this, similar types of accommodation in Bulgaria are concentrated near the Black Sea – admittedly in

Sveti Konstantin, one of the smaller Black Sea resorts, where the wide range of hotels includes the large and luxurious Grand Varna

places like quaint Nesebur and Sozopol, but also in purpose-built developments which may be attractive but lack historical 'roots' and traditional local identity.

CULTURE AND ENTERTAINMENT

Bulgaria's cultural traditions date back to the legends of Orpheus with his lyre and the amazing artistry of the Thracians who fashioned some of the world's earliest gold ornaments. Archaeology is very professionally pursued, incidentally. Exciting finds of artefacts in recent decades have achieved fame in touring exhibitions. A recent discovery, in 1986, was the Treasure of Rogozen, its ornate Thracian militaria now being distributed to big-city museums.

There are obviously impressive budgets for the conservation of architecture and art works from early medieval times, of monasteries and their icons, of whole villages and town centres with their National Revival buildings.

On the 'live' scene, there are about a million drama and opera performances annually in Bulgaria, and the nation's leading singers star in the world's greatest opera houses. All the larger Bulgarian cities have symphony orchestras, opera houses, theatres, cultural centres, museums and amateur

art companies.

Folk music and dance traditions flourish probably more than in any other European country. But national and international rock and pop have a more contemporary sound than many may expect, and bands in hotels and restaurants are very versatile. The same radio channel may broadcast pop and 'serious' music, and its producers (rightly, it seems) assume that young people are capable of appreciating both.

WEATHER AND WHEN TO GO

The climate is temperate continental with a Mediterranean influence in the southern regions. Mountain climate prevails in highland regions with altitudes of more than 3,000ft (900m). In the east of Bulgaria the climate is milder because of the influence of the Black Sea, and winter temperatures may be as high as 58°F (15°C), while the

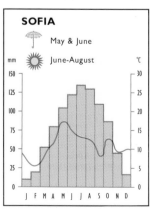

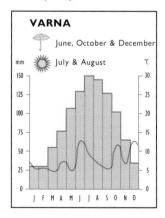

Keeping the tradition alive: thousands of singers and dancers at a folk festival in Sofia

summer temperatures rarely exceed 77–78°F (25–26°C). Water temperature in summer is between 65 and 77°F (17–25°C).

HOW TO BE A LOCAL

Since 1989 there have been many changes in Bulgaria, some of which affect tourists. It has become much easier to travel independently as small private hotels have opened up, and the pleasure of eating out has increased with the wider choice of cafés and restaurants. Although Bulgarians are famously hospitable and generous to a fault, there was in the past no real tradition of service, so that hotel receptionists, shop assistants and waiters were not always helpful or polite. Now the situation is much improved, and is getting better all the time. Confusion can still be caused by traditional body language, which is sometimes the opposite of ours. Shaking the head normally means 'yes', and nodding means 'no'. However, in Sofia, and with those used to dealing with foreigners, you may find that people adopt the western way, so be careful!

Visitors are still something of a novelty away from the main tourist areas, but the stares you receive are curious rather than hostile.

● If you intend leaving the beaten track, bring camera film, but it is now available in Sofia, major towns and along the coast.

● Carry tissues or toilet paper with you; it is not always available at roadside stops.

● Bring any special medicines, tampons and sanitary towels with you if you need them.

● If you like milk in hot drinks, bring a powdered supply. Bulgarians normally drink both tea and coffee black. Tea will often be herbal, and always weak for British tastes.

● A few areas will have signs forbidding photography; abide by these rules.

● Nude bathing is permitted on certain designated beaches. Topless sunbathing is accepted everywhere.

● Only exchange currency at hotels or exchange bureaux. The rates offered by street touts are rarely much better than official places, and such deals are risky.

Tourists unfamiliar with Cyrillic script might find they have been given a bundle of worthless dinars from former Yugoslavia, and not leva at all. Keep receipts, and you can change your remaining leva for sterling as you leave the country.

● If you are travelling independently, keep the *Carte Statistique* you get at the airport, and be sure to get it stamped each night wherever you stay. It must be handed in at passport control on departure.

● It is worth bringing a few small gifts from home to give away. Visitors invariably find themselves on the receiving end of Bulgarian hospitality, and it is nice to have something with which to reciprocate.

Pamporovo, in the Rhodope mountains, a resort for skiers of all ages and abilities

EVENTS

January

Winter sports competitions and carnivals in the ski resorts of

Borovets, Pamporovo and Cherni Vrukh; Plovdiv Winter Music Festival

February
'Vinegrowers' Day', folklore in wine districts on the 14th of the month.

March
Ruse International Music Festival

April
Bulgarian Music Days, Plovdiv

May
Plovdiv Spring Fair (consumer goods); Gabrovo Biennial Festival of Humour and Satire, every odd-numbered year
24 May – 20 June: Sofia Music Weeks, leading international festival

June
Rose Festival, Valley of Roses, Kazanluk; Golden Orpheus Pop Festival, Sunny Beach, every two years

June/July
Summer International Music Festival in Varna and Golden Sands

July
International Ballet Competition, Varna

August
Burgas International Folk Festival; sailing regatta, Duni, near Sozopol

September
Plovdiv Autumn Fair (machinery and technical equipment), and biennially Plovdiv Old Town Arts Festival; Sozopol Arts Festival

November
Katya Popova Laureate Days, Pleven; Jazz Parade, Sofia

December/January
Sofia International New Year's Music Festival.

CHILDREN

Bulgaria's Black Sea resorts have gone to imaginative lengths to offer children attractions in addition to their clean, sandy beaches and safe bathing in clear, tideless sea. Trained staff will look after them and keep them amused for hours when parents want a break.
● For children aged between two and twelve there are reductions on some holiday prices.
● Hotels ensure an extra bed in the parents' room, and a separate room for two children.
● Restaurants offer special children's menus with popular preferences, at special prices.
● Kindergartens open round the clock.
● Qualified nannies organise special activities for children.
● Excursion programmes provide entertainment for adults and children alike.
These are some facilities especially appealing to children at the three main resorts:

Sunny Beach (Slunchev Bryag)
There are playgrounds with slides, climbing frames and swings in front of the Iskur Hotel, near Lazur discothèque, outside the Neptune and Ribarska Hisha restaurants. Swimming pools in front of the Neptune and Ribarska Hizha restaurants; mini-golf in front of the Strandja, Iskur, Yantra and Sever Hotels; water slide outside the Zheravi Hotel; kindergartens, karting, puppet theatre, etc.
Bicycles and rickshaws near the

CHILDREN

Albena, a resort that has plenty on offer for the young

hotels Belassitsa, Strandja, Iskur. Continental, Sirena, Amphora and Kouban, as well as in the vicinity of the open-air theatre. Video games at the bowling centre.

Every week Balkan Holidays organises children's festivals at Bar Rusalka and Bar Astoria, camp fire sessions, child discos at the Rusalka café. There are donkey safaris in the forest, contests for the finest sandcastle, contests for the best asphalt drawing.

Excursions to Varna include visits to the dolphinarium, aquarium and zoo, scooter, transmobile and bobsleigh rides.

Golden Sands (Zlatni Pyasutsi)

Attractions for children here include the water slide outside the Metropol Hotel; two swimming pools in front of the Havana and Metropol Hotels;

karting next to the Zlatna Kotva Hotel, electric train next to the Zlatna Kotva Hotel; tennis school behind the Lilia Hotel.

Bicycles – in the resort centre, next to the Rodina, Malina and Havana Hotels; at Druzhba resort near Chernomorets restaurant and Grand Hotel Varna. Rickshaws and pedalos at South, North and Central beach. Kindergarten at the Strandja Hotel; video games at the bowling centre, at the Moskva and Strandja Hotels.

Balkantourist organises matinées with video films at the Shipka and Ambassador cafeterias.

Special programmes are at the Chaika children's club; drawing on asphalt, painting, contests and games, puppet shows, study of Bulgarian songs and dances.

Visit to the zoo in the town of Aitos.

Competitions with roller skates, sack races, boat rides; courses in riding, swimming, tennis,

waterskiing; trained instructor's programme adapted to children.

Albena

At Albena there is a water slide, a mini-train on the street, children's beach-karting, pedaloes, an air castle, paddling pools at the Tervel, Kaliakra and Kim Hotels; karting near Sever bazaar, next to the Cultural and Information Centre and near the Tervel and Kaliopa Hotels.

Mini-golf near the Kaliopa and Kardam Hotels, video games at Sever bazaar and near the Information Centre; there are donkey carts at the Slavyanka Hotel. There is also a Kiddie Kastle in front of the Dobrudza Hotel; kindergartens. Balkantourist organises children's festivals, contests and competitions, films and swimming lessons.

There is also a children's play corner at the Information Centre.

TIGHT BUDGET

Favourable exchange rates make virtually the whole country a 'bargain basement' for the holiday-maker and especially welcome for those on a tight budget. This can make a three-course meal and good bottle of wine in an attractive restaurant seem incredibly cheap to the westerner. And quite edible/drinkable fare can become progressively cheaper at a tavern called a *mehana*, or a *hanche*.

Snack bars and street vendors sell even cheaper take-away food, typically *kebapcheta* (mini mince rissoles) and *banitsa*, a savoury pastry that is usually made with cheese.

Many children's amusements come free of charge (or for just a few leva) in the seaside resorts, but be prepared to pay extra for evening baby-sitting services.

Museum charges tend to be nominal and, in cities like Varna and Ruse, seats at the opera are ridiculously cheap.

For the independent traveller, accommodation prices are also low, even in top-ranking 4- and 5-star hotels in the capital, where the most you can pay for a double room is about £55 ($80).

Private lodgings are very economically priced at around £7 ($10) for bed and breakfast per night.

Camping costs vary, depending on amenities, but around £7 ($10) should cover chalet accommodation (see also **Camping** in the **Directory** section, page 111).

Traditional cuisine includes such dishes as stuffed peppers and vine leaves, meatballs and hotpots

DIRECTORY

Arriving

By Air

The national carrier Balkan Bulgarian Airlines has four scheduled direct flights a week from London Heathrow to Sofia. Its offices in Britain are at 332 Regent Street, London W1 (tel: 071 637 7637); ticket sales are handled by Trade Winds, Morley House, Room 18, 5th Floor, 320 Regent Street, London W1 (tel: 071 631 1840). Balkan Air in New York is at 41 East 42nd Street, Suite 500, NY 10017 (tel: 212 573 5530).

There are also indirect flights via Amsterdam, Athens, Paris, etc. International airlines fly into Sofia from over 40 cities, and during the summer season direct flights also operate to Varna and Burgas from selected cities. Sofia airport is about 8 miles (13km) northeast of the city. The complex includes a Balkantourist office, restaurant, pharmacy, post office and money exchange. The city centre is reached either by bus (journey time about half an hour) or by taxi.

By Rail

Long-haul trans-European trains arrive in Sofia at the Central Station, a short tram ride from the city centre. Station facilities include a pharmacy, Balkantourist office and eateries. For rail information in the UK call Continental Train Enquiries on 071 834 2345, or contact Thomas Cook European Timetable, 0733 63200. In Sofia, book international tickets at the Rila travel office on General Gurko Street (see **Public Transport**).

By Road
Motorists enter the country via any of the 24 border checkpoints, where their cars will be registered. These include Kulata (on the border with Greece), Kapitan Andreevo (Turkish border), Vidin and Ruse (Romania) and several on the border with the former Yugoslavia. (see **Driving**).

Entry Formalities
British citizens visiting Bulgaria on package holidays and individuals travelling with vouchers for prepaid tourist services need only their 10-year passports. Independent travellers also need a visa. Though British passport holders can obtain a visa at the Bulgarian border, it is better to apply for one in advance at the Visa Section of the Bulgarian Embassy, 186 Queen's Gate, London SW7 8NA (tel: 071 584 9400); it takes about seven working days to come through and costs £20.
(If you are travelling through other countries en route to Bulgaria, you should also check with their embassies about necessary documentation).
Regulations in all Eastern European countries are currently subject to change; always check on the latest developments before you travel.

Camping
There are over 100 campsites around Bulgaria, though most are concentrated in the Black Sea tourist areas. Amenities vary considerably from bungalow-type accommodation to sites where you provide your own tent. Camping on unauthorised sites is illegal.

Chemist (see **Pharmacies**)

Crime
As Communism has fallen, so petty crime has risen, though Bulgaria is still relatively safe compared to western countries. Tourists, with obviously more money than the locals, may be targets for pickpockets so keep cash and credit cards in a money belt. Most hotels can keep your valuables in their safes for a small charge. Always lock your car, and your luggage as well, if possible; in any case keep an eye on bags at all times. Steer clear of black-marketeers and dubious money-exchange merchants. Take out adequate insurance before you travel.

Customs Regulations
You can import for your personal use 1 litre of spirits, 2 litres of wine, 250 cigarettes (or 250g of other tobacco products) and 50 grams of perfume. It is a good idea to declare valuable items such as cameras and camping on entry, to avoid problems when you leave. Keep all receipts for items bought while in Bulgaria to produce for customs if necessary.

Disabled Visitors
The facilities for visitors with mobility, visual or other disabilities, or those on a special (or even strictly vegetarian) diet, are not numerous in Bulgaria. Public transport is not adapted for wheelchairs, nor are most hotels and restaurants. Check

DIRECTORY

with your tour operator before booking. For up-to-date information on accommodation, transport and other aspects of travel contact (in Britain) the Holiday Care Service (0293 774535) or Radar (071 637 5400).

Driving

Main national roads include the E80, from Sofia to Kapitan Andreevo, passing through Plovdiv; the E79 from the capital down to Kulata by way of Blagoevgrad; the E87 which runs down the Black Sea side of the country, linking Durankulak, Varna and Malko Turnovo; the E70, from Ruse on the Romanian border, to Varna.

Accidents and Breakdowns

In case of a breakdown, call the local company representative if you are driving a hire car, or 146 for assistance from the Union of Bulgarian Motorists. In Sofia, the Union has offices at 3 Positano Place (tel: 02 883978) and 6 Sveta Sofia (tel: 02 470111). There are local offices throughout the country. The number for the traffic police is 166. Motorists must, by law, report accidents to the police.

Alcohol

Driving after alcohol consumption – irrespective of quantity – is strictly prohibited and there are heavy penalties if you are caught.

Car Rental

International companies, like Hertz and Europcar, have outlets in Sofia (at the airport and city centre hotels), Plovdiv, Ruse and other centres, including the Black Sea resorts. The minimum driving age is 21 years. Book in

advance (in Britain) by calling Hertz on 081 679 1799, Europcar 081 950 5050, or via their respective agents – Balkantourist and Interbalkan – in Bulgaria.

Fuel

Petrol stations are at an average of 18 to 25 miles (30 to 40km) apart on main roads. Lead-free fuel is available at very few stations. Filling stations are open usually from 06.00 to 22.00. In some places fuel vouchers are used rather than cash to pay for fuel. They are available at tourist offices, hotels, etc.

Insurance

Third party liability insurance, plus a green card, is obligatory; make sure that you are covered before you leave home. A visitor may drive on a current domestic licence.

Road Signs

These conform to international conventions and are therefore easily recognisable. Major towns are signed in both Cyrillic and Latin letters.

Speed Limits

For cars, the limit is 74mph (120kph) on motorways, 50mph (80kph) outside populated areas and 37mph (60kph) in populated areas.

Traffic Rules

Drive on the right; the wearing of seat belts is compulsory.

Electricity

Voltage is 220–240 AC; a continental adaptor is needed for the two-pin sockets

Embassies
Great Britain

65 Tolbukhin Boulevard, Sofia,

tel: 02 885361, 02 878325. The British embassy also looks after the interest of nationals of Australia, New Zealand and Canada.

USA
1a Stamboliiski Boulevard, Sofia, tel: 02 884801/5.

Emergency Telephone Numbers
Ambulance 150
Fire 160
Police 160, 166
Road Service 146
Telephone Information 144

Entry Formalities (See Arriving)

Health
Visitors are recommended to check that their immunisations against hepatitis A, polio and typhoid are up to date. There is a network of hospitals and polyclinics.
Charges are made for any medicines prescribed; reciprocal agreements exist with some countries for accident and emergency treatment. Check with the authorities in your own country before you travel.
It is vital you make sure you are adequately insured to cover any medical bills which may be incurred abroad.
In Sofia, the Clinic for Foreign Citizens is at Mladost 1, 1 Evgeni Pavlovski Street, tel: 02 75361.
Bulgaria abounds in health spas – there are over 600 springs in the country with temperatures ranging from a cool 10°C to a hot 102°C. You can take the cure (under medical supervision) with treatments including swimming, massage, acupuncture, saunas, solaria, infra-red and mud treatments. Before starting a course, a case history and medical diagnosis must be presented to the centre you are attending. If you are taking a baby, also take a supply of baby food, powdered milk and nappies.

Holidays (Public)
January 1 New Year
March 3 Day of Liberation from Turkish rule
Easter Sunday and Monday Orthodox church dates, variable
May 1–2 International Labour Day
May 24 Day of Bulgarian Culture
December 25 Christmas

Media
British newspapers are often

Hrelyo's defence tower at Rila Monastery

available from a kiosk in front of the University in Sofia and at the Sheraton Hotel Balkan, while tabloids are available at some Black Sea resorts. If you are desperate for news in English, try the libraries in major cities for periodicals such as the *International Herald Tribune*. In Varna, the Sofia Press Agency has Bulgarian newspapers translated into English.

There are two Bulgarian television channels, though some foreign stations may also be available. On the radio you can pick up the BBC World Service and, in Sofia and Varna, the Voice of America. Varna has its own English-language station.

Money Matters

The basic monetary unit is the lev (plural leva) subdivided into 100 stotinki (singular stotinka). Coins of 1, 2, 5, 10, 20 and 50 stotinki as well as of 1, 2 and 5 leva and notes of 1, 2, 5, 10, and 20, 50, 100 and 200 leva are in circulation. It is illegal to take Bulgarian currency into or out of the country. (Any left-overs must

Nesebur, a gem of a town

be traded in before departure). Exchange money at banks, bureaux de change, tourist offices or large hotels. Doing so outside such officially authorised exchanges is strictly prohibited and a punishable offence. When you change money, a receipt will be issued; keep this until you leave the country.

Credit cards accepted in Bulgaria are: American Express, Diners Club, Access, Mastercard and Visa. These are, in theory, accepted as payment for goods or services at over 500 places countrywide, including 250 hotels, Balkantourist offices, top restaurants and stores, car hire agencies and Balkan Airlines. However, never rely on your credit card being accepted; always check out the situation before committing yourself to goods or services.

Equally, beware of relying on travellers' cheques, especially outside major towns. They may not be accepted by hotels or tourist offices and you may not be able to find a bank which will accept them either.

Carry a mixture of credit cards, travellers' cheques and cash to be sure of paying your way.

Nudism
Nude sunbathing is forbidden in some areas, sometimes by unequivocal signs (see the illustration, page 119). Some younger Bulgarians do cast aside inhibitions and traditions, but observe carefully what is happening on the local beach before committing yourself. Near Varna, the beach at Fichoza is favoured by local nudists. There are also places around Sozopol, Dyumi and further south with nudist beaches.

Opening Times
Usually **shops** are open Monday to Friday from 08.00 to 17.00, and on Saturday until 14.00, though many stay open until 19.00. In Sofia, Tsum, the Central Universal Shop and largest department store, stays open from 08.00 until 21.00 on weekdays. (Outside major towns, lunchtime closing operates).

Banks are open Monday to Friday from 08.00 to 15.00, with

DIRECTORY

a lunchtime closing from 12.30 to 13.00. On Saturdays, opening hours are from 08.00 to 14.00. **Office hours** are Monday to Friday, 09.00 to 17.30. Post office hours vary from place to place, those in larger towns stay open from early morning (around 07.00) until late evening (23.00) daily. On average, Monday to Saturday, 07.00 to 12.00 and 13.00 to 16.00 should find most **post offices** open. Telephone sections stay open later; in cities, there is often 24-hour opening. **Museums and other sights** have no uniform opening hours, but they nearly all close for two hours for lunch.

Personal Safety

As in almost every country, single women travellers may attract unwanted attention; in provincial areas trendy or revealing clothes will exacerbate the situation, so use common sense in a country that remains relatively new to mass tourism. Violent crime against individuals is no worse than in Western Europe (but see **Crime** above). Before travelling to Bulgaria, visitors can ring their tour operator or government authorities for information on any local problems which might threaten their safety.

Pharmacies

Pharmacies may be able to help with minor ailments but are unlikely, certainly outside major resorts, to speak any English. In major towns – Sofia, Plovdiv, Ruse – there are 24-hour pharmacies. Medicines will be of non-western manufacture, so if you are on a course of treatment, ensure you take enough to last,

plus a doctor's prescription to validate the drugs.

Places of Worship

Burgas has both a Roman Catholic and an Orthodox church, and there is an Orthodox cathedral in Varna.

Police

The Bulgarian police, known as the **policija** (pronounced politzaiya), wear either a dark blue-grey or olive green uniform.

They can levy on-the-spot fines for traffic violations such as speeding and are very tough on drink/driving (see **Driving**) and drugs offences. It is fairly

*There is an abundant supply of
excellent fruits and vegetables*

unlikely the local policeman will
speak English.

Post Offices

Offices offering postal, telegraph
and telephone services can be
found in almost every town and
village and in holiday resort
complexes. Stamps can also be
bought at hotel reception desks.
The Central Post Office in Sofia,
on General Gurko Street, is open
until 20.30 (see **Opening Hours**)
and has Poste Restante facilities.
Mail to Europe can take up to
two weeks (longer to the US).

Public Transport
Air
Internal flights (Balkan Airlines)
operates between the capital
and Black Sea coast resorts
(served by Varna and Burgas
airports) and also some inland
destinations.

Balkan Airlines Offices:
Sofia: 12 Narodno Sabranie
Square (tel: 02 880663)
Burgas: Hotel Cosmos,
Osvoboditel Boulevard (tel: 056
34062)
Varna: 15 Boulevard K Boris, (tel:
052 442131/441811)

Buses
Tickets for buses, trams and
trolleybuses can be bought in
advance from the stations, kiosks
at stops, or from the driver.

Rail
Daily trains link Sofia with Varna,
Burgas, Ruse, and all other parts
of the country. Additional express
trains from Sofia to Varna and
Burgas run during the summer.
Railway booking offices handle
the advance sale of tickets and
seat reservations and provide
information:
Burgas, 106 Alexandrovska
Street, (tel: 056 23338)
Pleven, 2 Zamenhoff Street, (tel:
064 23756)
Plovdiv, 13 Gen Gurko Street,
(tel: 032 222729)
Ruse, 39 D Blagoev Street, (tel:
082 22845)
Sliven, 5 Kirkov Street, (tel: 044
3656)
Sofia, 23 Knyagainya Mariya
Luiza Boulevard, (tel: 02
870222); 8 Slaveikov Square,
(tel: 02 875742); in the underpass
of the National Palace of Culture
Varna, 10 Avram Gachev Street,
(tel: 052 223053)

DIRECTORY

Senior Citizens

Balkan Holidays runs special 'Over 55s' trips to a selection of Black Sea coast resorts (see **Tour Operators** below).

Student and Youth Travel

An International Student Identity Card entitles its holder to discounts on some local transport, entry fees to museums etc and entertainments. For details, contact your local student organisation or institution.

One calendar month's basic train travel, in 24 countries including Bulgaria is available with an InterRail Card. The card costs £249 and to qualify you must have been resident in the UK for six months. Ring Continental Train Enquiries on 071–834 2345 for further details.

(See also **Tourist Offices**).

Telephones

There are telephone booths at most post offices or dedicated central telephone offices where you make your call and pay your money afterwards. It is not possible to make reverse-charge calls in Bulgaria. In Sofia and other major tourist resorts there are also street kiosks which take 20 stotinki coins or phone cards. In theory it's possible to dial European numbers direct, but in some places you may have to wait half an hour for a connection.

To dial Bulgaria from the UK dial 010 359 followed by the area code (omitting the initial 0) and then the personal number. From the US, Canada and Australia dial 011 followed by the country code (359), the area and personal numbers. From New Zealand it's 00 followed by the

other three numbers. To dial the UK from Bulgaria dial 00, then 44 (the country code) then the area code, omitting the initial 0, then the subscriber number. For the US and Canada dial 00 1, for Australia 00 61 and for New Zealand 00 64.

Time

Local time is GMT plus two hours. Summer Time, (GMT plus three hours), lasts from the beginning of April until the end of September.

Tipping

This is not expected nor actively encouraged, but waiters, hotel staff, drivers and so on appreciate a 10 per cent tip.

Toilets

Keep plenty of small denomination notes handy as there is a small charge for the use of public toilets and those in hotels (even if you are staying there). Inflation has made the coinage almost worthless, and even toilets can cost one lev.

Tourist Offices

Balkantourist is the major tourist information agency in Bulgaria. (It is currently undergoing privatisation and may appear under different names in different places). It also arranges accommodation, acts as a currency exchange and car hire agent and gives information on travel in Balkan countries.

In Sofia, Balkantourist offices are at 1 Vitosa Boulevard, tel: 02 43331; fax: 80 01 34.

The Comprehensive Tourist Service office is at 37 Dondukov Boulevard, tel: 02 884430. They also have an office in the National Palace of

...except on designated beaches

Culture, tel: 02 597093.
The Orbita Youth Travel Agency,
which arranges accommodation
and holidays for young people,
is at 45A Stambolijiski Boulevard,
Sofia, tel: 02 801812/63939.
Information on youth hostels and
hiking is handled by the Pirin
Agency, 30 Stambolijiski
Boulevard, Sofia, tel: 02
870687/881079.
There are also tourist information
offices at the border checkpoints
at Durankulak, Kardam, Kulata,
Malko Turnovo, Gyueshevo,
Ruse, Kalotina and Kapitan
Andreevo.
The Bulgarian Tourist Office in
London is at 18 Princes Street,
W1R 7RE, tel: 071 499 6988.

Travel Agencies
Balkan Holidays 19 Conduit
Street, London W1R 9TD (tel: 071
493 8612).
Enterprise Groundstar House,
London Road, Crawley, West
Sussex RH10 2TB (tel: 0293
560777).
ACE Study Tours Babraham,
Cambridge CB2 4AP (tel: 0223
835055). Special-interest tours
with an educational theme on
history and architecture, ecology
and wildlife.
British Bulgarian Society c/o
Finsbury Library, 245 St John
Street, London EC1 4NB
(tel: 071 837 2304). Organises
holidays with special focuses on
botany, embroidery and textiles,
ornithology and many other
topics.

LANGUAGE

Useful Words and Phrases

Times, Dates and Numbers

what is the time? kólko e chasút?
when kogá?
today dnes
tomorrow útre
soon skóro
yesterday vchéra
Sunday Nedélya
Monday Ponedélnik
Tuesday Vtórnik
Wednesday Sryáda
Thursday Chetvúrtuk
Friday Pétuk
Saturday Súbota
this week tázi sédmitsa
next week slédvashtata
    sédmitsa
last week mínalata sédmitsa
spring próllet
summer lyáto
autumn éssen
winter zíma

1	ednó
2	dve
3	tri
4	chétiri
5	pet
6	shest
7	sédem
8	óssem
9	dévet
10	désset
11	edináyset
12	dvanáyset
13	trináyset
14	chetirináyset
15	petnáyset
16	shestnáyset
17	sedemnáyset
18	ossemnáyset
19	devetnáyset
20	dváyset
21	dváyset i ednó
30	tríyset
40	chetiríyset
50	petdessét
60	shéyset
70	sedendessét
80	ossemdessét
90	devetdessét
100	sto
500	pétstotin
1000	hílyada

January Yanuári
February Fevruári
March Mart
April Apríl
May Mai
June Yúni
July Yúli
August Avgúst
September Septémvri
October Októmvri
November Noémvri
December Dekémvri

Basics

welcome dobré doshli
good morning dobró útro
good day (used after about
    10am) dóbur den
good evening dóbur vecher
good night léka nosht
hello zdraveí (singular and
    familiar form)
    zdravéite (plural and polite
    form)
please mólya
thank you blagodaryá, mercí
you're welcome nyáma zashtó
excuse me/I am sorry izvinéte
congratulations moite
    pozdravleniya
how are you? kak ste?
very well, thank you blagodryá,
    mnógo dobré
do you speak Bulgarian/
    English/French/German/
    Russian?/ govórite li
    búlgarski/anglíski/
    frénski/némski/rúski?
I speak a little Bulgarian

govórya málko búlgarski

do you understand? razbírate li?

I do not understand ne vi razbíram

please speak more slowly govoréte po-bávno

please write it down bihte li me napísali

what's this called kak se kazva tova?

yes da

no ne

where are you going? kudé otívate?

I am going to the seaside otívam na moré

Worn with pride by young and old; national costumes are vibrant with colour, rich in embroidery

I am going to the mountains otívam na planiná

I am interested in the history of Bulgaria interesuvam se ot istóriyata na Bulgáriya

I am going to tour the countryside shte obikolyá stranáta

have a nice time priyátno prekárvane

pleased to meet you priyátno mi e da se zapoznáya s vas

meet my husband/wife zapoznáite se s móya suprúg/móyata / suprúga

how do you do priyátno mi e

what is your name? kak se kázvate?

my name is... kázvam se...

what country do you come from? otkudé ste?

I come from Great Britain/
England /Scolland/Wales/
Ireland az sum ot
Velikobritániya/Ángliya/
Shotlándiya/ Uéls/Irlándiya

are you married? zhénen li ste?

no, I am single ne, ne sum
zhenen

I hope I'll see you again
nadyávam se da se
vídim pak

so do I az sushto

when can I see you again?
kogá shte vi vidya otnóvo?

here you are zapovyádaite

you are very kind mnógo ste
lyubézen (to a man)
lyubézna (to a woman)

goodbye dovizhdane

all the best vsíchko nái-húbavo

Travel

how can I get to the airport? kak
móga da otída do letíshteto?

**where is the departure point for
the airport buses?** otkudé
trúgvat avtobúsite
za letíshteto?

**what time does the next bus
leave/arrive?** kogá trúgva/
pristíga slédvashtiyat
avtobús?

how much does it cost? kolko
struva tova?

bus avtobús

ticket bilét

porter nossách

where are our seats, please?
kudé sa ni mestáta, mólya?

here tuk

there tam

Troyan Monastery, the country's third largest, founded in 1600 and a centre of Bulgarian nationalism during Ottoman domination. Visitors can stay here if they wish

on the left-hand side v lyávo
on the right-hand side v dyásno
when will the plane take off?
    kogá izlíta saméta?
in ten minutes sled désset
    minúti
the plane is landing samolétat
    se prizemyáva
we had a very pleasant journey
    putúvaneto beshe mnógo
    priyátno
petrol station benzinostántsiya
please fill it up mólya, zaredéte
I have had a breakdown kolata

me se povrédi
where is the nearest service
    station? kudé e nai-blízkiya
    ávtoservíz?
I have a flat tyre spúkah gúma
I haven't got a spare tyre
    nyámam rezérvna gúma
I have lost my way sbúrkal sam
    pútya
which is the road to Sofia? koi e
    pútyat za Sófia?
Sofia is the capital of Bulgaria
    Sofia e stólitsa na Balgáriya
driving is on the right-hand side
    dvizhénieto e v dyásno
car park párking
free parking bezpláten párking
camping site kúmping
help! pomosht!
how far is it to...? kolko e dalech
    do...
where is... kudé se namira
please tell me... mozhe li da mi
    kázhete
how can I get there? kak moga
    da otida do tam?
which bus goes to the centre?
    s koi avtobús moga da otida
    v tséntura?
is this the bus/boat to... tózi li e
    avtobúsa/parahóda za...

Hotels

where is hotel...? kudé e
    hotél...?
a suite apartamént
a single room ediníchna stáya
a double room stáya s dvoino
    legló
a twin-bedded room stáya s
dva
leglá
an extra bed dopulnitelno legló
your room number is... vie ste
v   stáya nómer...
on the first floor na púrviya
    etázh
second vtóriya
third trétiya

LANGUAGE

fourth chetvúrtiya
fifth pétiya
sixth shéstiya
seventh sédmiya
eighth óssmiya
ninth devétiya
tenth dessétiya
the key, please klyúcha mólya
where is the toilet, please? kudé e toalétnata, mólya?
is there a hairdressers near here? ima li friziórski salon nablízo?
there is a hairdressers in the hotel v hotéla ima friziórski salón
can I hire a car here? móga li da naéma kolá tuk?
yes, we have rent-a-car service da, imame sluzhba za kolí pod náem
where can I get a taxi? ima li taksíta nablízo?
will you please order me a taxi for tomorrow morning at 7 o'clock? bihte li mi porúchali taksí za útre
sutrintá v sédem chassá, mólya?
will you wake me at 7 o'clock? sabudéte me v sédem chassa, mólya?
where is the nearest restaurant? kudé e nai-blízkiyat restoránt?
is there any post for me? ima li póshta za men?
where can I buy stamps? kudé móga da kúpya póshtenski márki?
from the post office v póshtata
have you got a telephone directory? imate li telefónen ukazátel?
do you want to leave a message? da predám li néshto?
sorry, wrong number izvinéte, gréshka
please speak louder govoréte

pó-sílno mólya
please repeat again mólya povtoréte
I do not feel well ne sum dobré
have you anything for a headache? imate li néshto za glavobólie?
my wife/husband/child is not well zhená mi/muzhút mi/detéto mi ne e dobré
would you please send for the doctor mólya, povíkaite lékar
please may I have a map of the town/resort? mólya, dáite mi kárta na gradá/na kurórta?

museum muzéi
art gallery hudózhestvena galériya
exhibition izlózhba
open otvóreno
closed zatvóreno

Restaurants
restaurant restoránt
folk-style restaurant mehaná
do you have a table for 2, 3, 4? imate li mássa za dváma/tríma/chetiríma?
on the terrace na terássata
inside vútre
waiter servityór
may I have the menu, please? bihte li mi dáli menyúto, mólya?
knife nosh
fork vílitsa
spoon luzhítsa
napkin salfétka
plate chiníya
glass/cup chásha
may I have something to drink? mólya vi, néshto za píene?
yes, of course da, razbíra se
what would you like? kakvó zheláete?
tea chai
coffee kafé

wine   víno
soft drinks   bezalkohólni napítki
water   vodá
soda water   gazírana vodá
fruit juice   plódov sok
brandy   konyák
white wine   byálo víno
red wine   chervéno víno
dry/medium/sweet wine
   súho/polusúho/sládko víno
beer   bíra
cheers!   nazdráve!
tea with lemon/milk   chai s
   limón /mlyáko
black coffee   esprésso
white coffee   kafé s mlyáko
Turkish coffee   túrsko kafé
food   hraná
bread   hlyáb
toast   prepéchen hlyáb
butter   masló
eggs   yaitsá
sandwich   sándvich
salad   saláta
soup   súpa
fish   ríba
sugar   záhar
peppers   chúshki
tomatoes   domáti
cucumber   krástavitsa
vegetarian dishes   póstni yastiyá
meat dishes   yastiyá s mesó
grills   skára
omelette   omlét
salt   sol
pepper   chéren pipér
vinegar   otsét
yellow cheese   kashkavál
white cheese (like feta)   sírene
pudding   dessért
ice cream   sladoléd
yoghurt   kísselo mlyáko
apples   yábulki
strawberries   yágodi
pears   krúshi
cherries   cheréshi
raspberries   malíni
watermelon   dínyi
melon   púpesh

apricots   kaissí
peaches   práskovi
lemon   limón
grapes   grózde
Bulgarian food is very delicious
   Búlgarskata hraná e mnógo
   vkúsna
cigarettes   tsigári
matches   kibrít
do you smoke?   púshite li?
would you like a cigarette?
   zheláete li tsigára?
may I have the bill, please?
   smétkata, mólya?

*An old woman on the streets of Rila
threads leaves of tobacco, one of the
country's main products*

INDEX

Page numbers in *italics* refer to pictures

ACKNOWLEDGEMENTS

ACKNOWLEDGEMENTS

The Automobile Association would like to thank the following photographers and libraries for their assistance in the compilation of this book

J ALLAN CASH PHOTOLIBRARY 38 Rila Monastery, 67 Stone Forest, 78 folk dancing, 113 Rila Monastery, 125 old woman. D ASH 63 Shiroka Luka, 122/3 Troyan Monastery. P ATTERBURY Cover: Shipka Memorial Church, 7 nr Aitos, 9 Veliko Turnovo, 54 Shipka. 72 Nesebur, 119 notice, Sunny Beach. BULGARIAN TOURIST BOARD 4 nr Cape Kaliakra, 5 Location Map, 11 Archaeology Museum, Sofia, 23 Alexander Nevsky Mem. Church, 24 souvenirs, 26/7 Bulgarian cuisine, 27 restaurant, Sheraton Hotel, 29 Vitosha Hotel Shtastlivetza, 31 Samokov drinking fountain, 32 Ritlite Rocks, 34/5 Belogradchik Fortress, 36/7 Vidin, 40 Melnik, 43 Rila Mountains, 45 Khisar, 47 Plovdiv, 48 Plovdiv Roman Theatre, 51 Valley of the Roses, 52 Etura, 56 Veliko Turnovo, 58 Preslav, 60 Kotel monument, 61 Pamporovo, 62 Map, 68 The Black Sea, 69 Kamchiya, 70/1 Sozopol, 75 Hotel Varna, Druzhba, 76 Golden Sands, 80/1 Sunny Beach, 83 Pleven, 85 tomb mural at Kazanluk, 99 market, 100/1 Bulgarian dishes, 103 Druzhba, 105 singers, 106 Pamporovo, 108/9 Albena, 110 traditional food, 114/5 Nesebur, 116/7 market, 121 Pirin singers. MARY EVANS PICTURE LIBRARY 12 Surrender of Bulgarian Soldiers, 17 The National Liberation Movement. NATURE PHOTOGRAPHERS LTD 87 wildcat (W S Paton), 89 eagle owl (E A Janes), 90 white pelicans (R S Daniel), 93 ghost orchid, 95 gentiana (C Grey-Wilson), 96 wall lizard, 97 wood ants, 98 white stork (P R Sterry). ZEFA PICTURE LIBRARY (UK) LTD 19 Ivan Vasov Nat. Theatre, 64/5 Bachkovo Monastery.

AUTHOR'S ACKNOWLEDGEMENTS

David Ash wishes to thank the Bulgarian National Tourist Office, Balkantourist, the Bulgarian Association for Tourism and Recreation, Balkanair, and numerous guides for their help during visits over 26 years which enabled him to write this book. For incidental information, he is particularly grateful to Elisaheth Hussey of the Ski Centre of Great Britain, journalist Moira Rutherford, guide George Poshtov, and friends with 'Discover Bulgaria'. Thanks also to Dr Annie Kay, for her assistance on the 1994 revision.